YOUR CHILD'S
DEVELOPMENT
IN THE FIRST
FIVE YEARS

YOUR CHILD'S DEVELOPMENT IN THE FIRST FIVE YEARS

RONALD S. ILLINGWORTH

MD, FRCP, DPH, DCH
Emeritus Professor of Child Health, The University of Sheffield;
Formerly Paediatrician to the Children's Hospital, Sheffield

CHURCHILL LIVINGSTONE
EDINBURGH LONDON MELBOURNE AND NEW YORK 1981

CHURCHILL LIVINGSTONE
Medical Division of Longman Group Limited

Distributed in the United States of America by
Churchill Livingstone Inc., 19 West 44th Street, New York,
N.Y. 10036, and by associated companies,
branches and representatives throughout
the world.

First published 1981

ISBN 0 443 02237 2

British Library Cataloguing in Publication Data
Illingworth, Ronald Stanley
Your child's development in the first five years.
— (Patient handbooks).
l. Child development
I. Title   II. Series
155.4'22   BF721   80—40744

Printed in Singapore by Singapore Offset Printing Pte Ltd

PREFACE

Nearly all babies are born in working order: but all babies and children are different — different in their personality, behaviour, physical growth and mental development — and so in the age at which they begin to smile at their mother, to use their hands, to play, sit, walk, talk and control the bladder. These differences, not amounting to disease, and not suggesting abnormality, cause anxiety and worry mothers. There are big babies and little babies, of the same age; there are thin children and fat children; bad tempered babies and placid easy going ones; quiet babies and noisy babies and children who are always on the go. Some cry excessively; some won't eat; some won't sleep; some won't use the pottie. Almost all are determined from the age of one to three, to do the opposite of what the mother wants them to do. Some are real tyrants; they know exactly what they want and how to get it. They are all different. All children (and all parents, and all teachers), have behaviour problems: some of these nearly drive the mother to distraction.

The more parents know the normal, the normal behaviour problems, the normal variations in behaviour, in physical growth and in development, the better. Not only does a knowledge of the normal help a mother to understand her child and to cope with the various problems as they arise: but knowledge of the normal helps a mother to observe the fascinating process of the development of the human mind. It helps her to enjoy her baby and child to the full, and to understand him better.

This book is designed to provide mothers in entirely non-technical language with a brief account of the normal child's development — emotional (behaviour), physical and mental or intellectual. It discusses the many factors which affect his development, laying particular emphasis on the part which parents play in helping him to use his talents to the full, and more than that, to be a nice person and so to achieve the best of which he is capable. His emotional, physical and mental development are intimately related and this book is intended to guide parents in the management of all three of those aspects of development in his first five years in their aim to bring the best out of their child.

Sheffield, 1980   R.S.I

CONTENTS

4. How should he develop mentally? /37

1. INTRODUCTION

Most parents want to do their best for their child: they want him to be a success in life; some want him to be a genius; some want him to be perfect, a model of virtue; some fathers want him to do as well as they did, or better; but none of us know how to achieve all this. None of us know the answer to all the problems of childhood: none of us know with certainty how to help a child to achieve his best. All that we can do is to try to profit from our own experience, to profit from the experience of others, to try to understand, at least in part, the workings of the human mind, to learn about the normal child, his development, the factors affecting it, some harmful, some helpful, and the ways of helping him — put all this together, and do our best. We shall try to avoid the mistakes which we think that our parents made: but then we shall make new ones which they avoided. None of us are perfect, and neither will our children be.

The more we can know about and understand the normal development of the human mind, the more we can help it. It is essential that you should know your child's basic needs — for love and security, physical health, wise loving discipline, a good example as a model, and the gradual achievement of independence. Physical, emotional and intellectual development are closely interlinked: we cannot hope that our child will achieve his best intellectually unless we attend to both his emotional and physical needs.

2. HOW SHOULD HE DEVELOP EMOTIONALLY?

A child's personality, like his intelligence, is partly inherited and partly the product of his environment and upbringing. The development of his personality is related to his general development, which in turn is largely related to his intelligence. For example, whereas it is normal for a child of 2 or 3 to cling to his mother and to be reluctant to be separated from her, as he matures he is able more and more to tolerate separation, so that he can go to school: but a mentally backward child, who will be later than others in maturing, will be later in tolerating such separation. Whereas most normal small children are highly active and always 'on the go', (and are often called 'overactive'), they mostly grow out of this as they mature, but children with a lower than average level of intelligence are later than others in losing their 'overactivity'. But underlying personality features are also relevant to the age at which the excessive clinging or overactivity are lost.

Children express displeasure long before they express pleasure: they cry before they begin to smile. They learn to say 'no' before they say 'yes'.

Personality development

At about 5 or 6 months of age children begin to show signs of their developing ego. They begin to show likes and dislikes:

they fuss when certain foods are offered; they cry when a toy is removed; they may fuss if prevented from trying to hold a spoon or cup or bottle. By 9 or 10 months they characteristically repeat a performance which you have laughed at. At this stage they are entirely selfish: they know what they want and see no reason why they should not have it.

Soon they show the development of the normal negativism which is a feature of the 1 to 3-year-old: they always seem to want to do the opposite of what they are asked to do. They want to be recognised as persons of importance, as individuals. If you want your child to go out, he wants to stay in; if you want him to put a coat on, he refuses; if you want him to take a particular food, he rejects it; if you try to make him eat more, he refuses; if you try to make him use the pottie, he will violently object; if you want him to go to sleep, he will stay awake, though obviously tired. He loves the fuss and attention he is causing. If he can get the whole house revolving around what he eats, or what he does in the pottie, or about his going to sleep, he will greatly enjoy the whole thing. If you have a fight with him about anything he will win. If you make determined efforts to stop him sucking his thumb or biting his nails, it will inevitably continue as a way of attracting attention. If you try to stop his tics (facial twitches, gaping, shoulder shrugging, etc.) it will certainly make them worse.

It is an exceedingly trying time for mothers — but far less trying if you understand that it is normal, that all children at this age are nonconformists, but that they will grow out of it — at least until puberty. If you know that it is normal, and can laugh at it, half the battle is won. Some children, simply because of their basic personality, are much more difficult to manage at this age than are other children. Unfortunately parents with a strong personality of their own, who were themselves really difficult to cope with in their own childhood, are likely to have the most difficult children. It is the placid, easy-going parents who are likely to have placid children who are easy to manage. Fortunately children become much easier to manage by about 3. Parents should take heart in the thought that the truly impossible toddler of today is likely to grow up to be a delightful adult.

Bound up with the development of the ego is the attention-seeking device. Children will try to attract attention by, for example, throwing temper tantrums, dirt eating and retching. This is best dealt with by being ignored, but unfortunately they cannot always be ignored: I saw a girl who, when thwarted, went into the kitchen and turned the gas tap on; I have seen boys who, when they know that they are being watched, eat snails or roundworms in the garden, or drink the drain water, or fill their mouths with pebbles. One small boy made his mother worried that he was becoming a sexual pervert by lifting ladies' skirts up.

New skills

Young children take great pleasure in practising their newly acquired skills. It satisfies their ego, their feeling of importance, if they can feed themselves, attend to their toilet needs, dress themselves, draw, fit interlocking bricks together or put the pyramid rings onto the stick. They enjoy their developing independence: and it is important to encourage this, to give them the means of looking after themselves, of learning from their new skills. The basis of the Montessori method of education is just this — to help them to learn when they are ready for it, as soon as they have developed the necessary ability or maturity. It gives them a sense of achievement, a feeling of importance. Soon they can be given responsibility — as in setting the table for a meal, helping to cook and prepare a meal, helping to wash up.

Habit formation

An important part of development is habit formation. Children from the age of 9 months or so readily acquire habits, good and bad: it is for the parents to try to prevent the development of bad habits. For instance, if you let your ten-month-old child learn that as soon as he calls out or cries after being put to bed, he will be taken downstairs again, he will call out every night. If he finds that if he cries when put to bed, you will return and sit at his bedside or even lie down at his side, he will demand it every night: if he finds that later on in the evening or night, as soon as he calls out, he will be taken into your bed, he will expect it and do it every night. The more intelligent the child the more rapidly will he learn how to control his environment in this way — how to get you to do what he wants you to do.

Habit formation arises from the conscious mind: it is deliberate. But 'conditioning' arises from the subconscious mind. If the child is smacked for not eating his dinner, or even repeatedly scolded for not eating, he begins to associate meal times with unpleasantness, and so refuses food. I saw a child who regularly cried as soon as a meal was ready; he knew that there was going to be unpleasantness. If a child is made to sit on his pottie when he wants to get off, or is smacked for not using it, he will learn to associate the eliminations with unpleasantness, and will refuse to part with his urine or stools. There will then be real trouble for his mother.

Set a good example

Children are imitators. Hence it is vital that in innumerable different ways you should set a good example. By the age of six months it is obvious that babies can imitate their parents by body movements — such as putting out the tongue, coughing, clapping their hands — but in fact they are able to imitate much earlier than this. As your child matures, it is vital that you should set a good example — of love, honesty, unselfishness, helpfulness, forgiveness, and kindness. The child will be influenced by what you say and do, by your manners, good and bad. If you ignore him when he speaks to you, or you show annoyance by his questions, or are otherwise rude to him, you must expect him to treat you in the same way. If you are always unselfish, do things for others which you would otherwise not want to do, if you take the lead where necessary, if you do things for people willingly and never grudgingly, if you are able to accept blame, to admit having made a mistake, to apologise for being unfair in a comment or act, or for losing your temper, you are likely to find that your child follows your example and grows up to do the same. If you never apologise for losing your temper, you cannot expect your child to do so either. If you show that you are willing to discuss matters when someone has disagreed with you, that you are able to change your mind and be persuaded to alter your viewpoint — other than to secure the other's approval — he benefits from your example.

If you are never heard to make unkind comments about people, or to make obviously irrational comments, but always are seen to look for the good in others, to look for possible excuses or reasons for their actions, he will be likely to follow your example. He should see your tolerance, sympathy, and thoughtfulness; he should see that you never harbour a grievance, that you try to help people you know and visit them when they are ill. If you are boastful, you must expect your child to be the same.

Children are greatly influenced by parental example in innumerable other ways. If two parents smoke, there is a considerable likelihood that their child will: if only one smokes, he is still likely to follow the example but less likely than the child both of whose parents smoke.

Children are influenced by the interests of their parents, so you can help their intellectual development by showing interest in as many things as possible.

Children are remarkably affected by the atmosphere in the home. They are seriously influenced by quarrelling, especially between their parents, or by drunken behaviour. I have known children develop acute asthma or acute abdominal pain or other symptoms when they have witnessed a quarrel between their mother and father. The bad psychological consequences to children of divorce have been shown to depend far more on the preceding domestic turmoil than on separation from one of the parents.

Children who never hear a cross word between mother and father are greatly helped with regard to their own personality — and with regard to the way in which they will bring up their own children. But it is not only parental discord which upsets children: a child is upset by constant discord between his parents and his brothers or sisters. The child is affected favourably or unfavourably by the whole atmosphere of the home. A happy home breeds happy children.

Children can be led

It is very easy to suggest dislikes or fears to children — just as it is sometimes easy to suggest that certain foods are nice. If you show fear of thunder or other loud noises, it is to be expected that your child will exhibit similar fears. Likewise, if you show that you do not like a particular type of food, your child may also decide not to like it.

Tall stories

As the small child matures, he becomes more imaginative. It is normal for a 2- or 3-year-old to have imaginary companions behind the sofa, and to indulge in fantasy thought and play. It is normal for small children — 4, 5, or 6 years old — to tell tall stories. It is easy for a mother to inhibit such fantasy thought and play, to ridicule it as being silly, or to regard it as lying. It is better to accept such play and conversation as normal and in no way to discourage it. It might well help to make your child creative, which may help the child greatly in years to come. I find it difficult to say in words at exactly what stage a mother has to draw the line between fantasy and untruthfulness. I suggest that when one is uncertain, one should give the child the benefit of the doubt: it must depend on the circumstances at the time. Parental example of honesty is essential for the child's upbringing.

Respect for the property of others

Just as it is difficult to draw the line between fantasy and untruth, so it is difficult to draw the line between the younger child's total disrespect for the property of others and theft. It is sensible to allow a child a box or cupboard for his own property — and to make it clear that it is his and no one else's. Gradually he learns that he cannot take toys or books from others without their permission. Parental example in this respect is most important: a child must never see one parent take the property of someone else nor must he hear a parent talking about some act of dishonesty or theft which he has committed.

Constant activity

Babies, children and adults differ widely in the degree of activity which they display. Some babies (especially the thin, wiry ones) are much more active than others (especially the fat, placid ones). Children at the age of 5, 6 or 7 seem to be always on the go, exhausting their parents, teachers and everyone else but themselves. Very many children in this age group find it impossible to walk sedately at their mother's side, holding her hand: they seem forced to hop and skip all the time. Neither can they sit still at the table: they constantly fidget, kicking table legs and human legs indiscriminately as they sit. Often they seem to require very little sleep — while the fat placid children who are far less active sleep far more. In the United States, and to a lesser extent in other 'developed' countries, children with excessive overactivity are often said to have 'minimal brain damage' with no evidence whatsoever to support the diagnosis of brain damage. There is in fact no psychological or clinical test which can provide evidence of 'brain damage'. Sometimes this excessive activity is associated with poor concentration, impulsive behaviour and other features. As they get older and mature the overactivity is usually lost: backward children lose the overactivity later than others.

All children are different; and in the great majority this excessive activity is merely normal, a feature of the personality. Very often it is an inherited feature — a grandparent exclaiming that the child's mother was exactly the same at that age. It can be a late result of the mother's smoking or alcohol excesses during pregnancy; it may be a feature of children in a house in which the parents smoke a great deal. It can result from excessive restrictions from boredom, insecurity, school difficulties, or domestic turmoil. It is an important side effect of several drugs, such as barbiturates or medicines used to prevent fits. It is possible that in some cases it is due to food additives, such as tartrazine, a yellow dye found in fruit drinks, many prepared foods and medicines, or to preservatives in foods.

Temper, fighting, quarrelling, aggressiveness

Displays of temper, aggresiveness, quarrelling or fighting are features of the normal developing child. Some children are much more troublesome than others; it depends partly on their personality. This may worry and annoy you if you do not realise how normal it is. Young children from 12 months or so of age, when thwarted and deprived of something which they want, or when another child takes a toy from them, are likely to scream, stamp their feet, and in a variety of ways show their strongest disapproval. Wherever possible you should ignore temper tantrums, for it is certain that they will continue and frequently recur if the child finds that he can attract attention, create fuss and anxiety, and end up by getting his own way if he has a really spectacular tantrum. But it is most disappointing for him if he puts a lot of energy into lying on the floor screaming and kicking, and no one pays any attention to him, so that he gets nothing out of it. It is just not worthwhile for him. Unfortunately it is not always easy to ignore tantrums: when a child takes a running kick at someone's rear quarters, or throws cups, knives and forks into the fire, it requires considerable parental control and imagination to cope with the situation.

Children learn a lot at home from fighting and quarrelling. They learn that they cannot have all their own way. It is far better for them to learn at home to live with others than to learn the hard way when they start school, as an only child often has to do. You should do your best to let your children find their own solution to their disagreements: you must resist the inevitable temptation to step in and stop their fights. But you have to step in when they are showing signs of doing definite harm to each other. When play is turning into a fight, you should attempt to distract the warring parties and change the subject.

It is difficult to know what to do if your child is unduly aggressive towards neighbours' children; but it is certain that if a boy's aggressiveness attracts a great deal of attention, and determined efforts are made to stop it, he will carry on behaving that way so as to attract more attention.

Both adults and children are inclined to be irritable and bad tempered if they are hungry, tired or bored. When a small child comes in from school in a bad temper, the unwise parent tries to reason with him, and when that fails gets annoyed, reprimands or punishes him: but the wise parent ignores his behaviour and rapidly gives him a meal, after which all is well. You should expect your small child to be impossible when he is hungry, tired or unwell: and do not be surprised if he has moods, like you do, with days when everything seems to be wrong.

Jealousy, fears, timidity, shyness

All children are jealous, and unless parents realise that this is normal, they may be worried and upset by the child's irrational behaviour and wonder what they have done wrong to make him behave in that way. Jealousy represents a child's feeling that he has lost his feeling of importance — as when a brother or sister comes on the scene — or feels that his brother or sister has something which he would like. The narrower the age gap between children the greater the likelihood of jealousy; the wider the gap the less the reason for jealousy.

The signs may be obvious — the boy may scream when his sister is picked up, or he may hit her on the head. But the jealousy may be subconscious and the signs of it much less obvious — as when he becomes suddenly more aggressive, wants to be fed when he can perfectly well feed himself, begins to soil or wet his pants, or shows other undesirable behaviour. Punishment will inevitably make him worse, for he will then become all the more certain that he has lost your love. What he wants is love, a feeling of being wanted, of being important. Instead of scolding him go out of your way to show him love, to make him feel more secure, more important.

All young children develop fears and shyness, especially from 12 months onwards. Coyness in the presence of strangers, fears of loud noise, of going down the hole in the bath, fear of dogs, are all normal. They must never be ridiculed for they are genuine and are simply features of their developing mind. It is stupid to say 'don't be shy', 'don't be afraid'; they cannot help it. Neither can some children avoid undue timidity. It is a feature of their personality; but they can be helped to some extent to learn to defend themselves.

Body manipulations

By the term 'body manipulations' I mean thumb-sucking, nail biting, nose picking, rocking in bed, head rolling, head banging, hair plucking, ear pulling, lip sucking, tongue sucking, tooth grinding, and masturbation. Some of these are indulged in by all children: some of them upset mothers and fathers — though they did them themselves. It seems surprising that some mothers are disturbed when their baby sucks his thumb and they try to stop it: but all babies do it and it is harmless — though it may occasionally make the thumb, finger or wrist sore, according to which part they suck. Babies suck their thumb or wrist while still in their mother's womb — and occasionally a baby is born with a blister on the hand as a result. One often sees the child put his thumb or fingers into his mouth when he is tired, hungry or feeling coy in the presence of strangers. Children get out of it as they mature: only very rarely it persists beyond the age of 6 or 7, and then occasionally it causes deformity of the teeth.

About half of all children bite their nails at some stage. A few pick their nails. Some girls bite their toe nails. Nail biting characteristically develops at the age of 8 to 10: it is rare before the age of 3. It may arise partly as a result of imitation. Children and adults often bite their nails when feeling tense. Efforts to stop it will cause it to continue as an attention-seeking device.

It is common for the baby at 6 months or so to rock on hands and knees in bed. It is common for babies to roll their head — often producing a bald patch on the back of the head. All these practices are harmless: and determined efforts to stop them will inevitably encourage the child to continue them in order to gain attention.

Head banging is an annoying habit, commonly resulting from a feeling of insecurity: the child bangs his head on the floor, or against the table, or more commonly against the end of the bed at night. It is harmless but annoying. It is particularly common between the ages of 7 and 12 months.

Some children, mainly when feeling insecure, pull their hair out, or pluck the hair or wool from blankets or clothes.

Tooth grinding is common in sleep, and is of no significance.

Almost all children sooner or later masturbate, some more than others. It is normal for the boy to handle his penis. It should on no account be discouraged. A small girl may sit astride the arm of a chair and rock back and forth, going red in the face: either it should be ignored, or an attempt should be made to distract her. These practices are harmless: but if you display anxiety about them, punish or reprimand the child, and try to reason with the child, they will continue as an attention seeking device. When it is excessive, it is commonly a manifestation of insecurity.

Tics and stuttering

Tics or habit spasms are common in young children, usually starting at the age of 6 or 7. They consist of blinking the eyes, twitching of the face, sniffing, coughing, shoulder shrugging or inappropriate mouth opening or gaping. They arise from the subconscious mind, and are commonly a feature of insecurity. Efforts to stop the tic by reprimands can only prolong the tic, make the child selfconscious and lead to unpleasantness. Most of them disappear after a few months.

Stuttering (which is the same as stammering) is a complex problem, often running through a family. It is normal for a 3-year-old to repeat syllables, especially when he is excited, and to stumble over words. It is vital then that this speech hesitancy should be ignored, for efforts to get the child to 'speak clearly and distinctly', to 'say it again', to 'think before speaking' will inevitably make the child selfconscious and begin true stuttering. Only if it is severe by the age of 3½ to 4 years should the possibility of speech therapy be raised. Treatment should not be postponed after that.

Basic needs for his emotional development

Love and security

All children need to be loved, to feel loved, to be wanted and to be secure from birth onwards. The importance of the establishment of a bond between mother and baby at birth and immediately after has attracted much recent attention in the United States and Scandinavia. In Britain it has for many years been the usual practice to hand the baby immediately at birth to the mother, and to keep the baby's crib at the mother's bed side so that she can pick him up and admire him whenever she wants, or whenever he cries, and feed him when he wants a feed. Throughout the animal kingdom the mother licks the newborn as soon as it is born: and throughout the animal kingdom if the newborn animal is removed from the mother immediately at birth so that she cannot lick it, and is then returned to the mother a few hours later, she rejects the animal. A goat for instance, would kick her kid to death when returned to her a few hours after birth, after she had been prevented from licking it. We have long known that when the naked newborn baby is placed on the mother's naked chest at birth, that mother is more likely to be able to breast feed her baby than a mother who does not experience this immediate contact.

Many mothers are afraid of spoiling their baby by picking him up. Do not be afraid of spoiling your child by loving him. You will spoil him by not giving him all the love that he wants. If you give him time in the early weeks, and respond to his cries to be picked up, he will be very much less trouble when he is older. Babies differ greatly in their demands: some want to be in their mother's arms for most of their waking hours; others demand this very little. Many mothers are afraid that there is something wrong with their baby who cries incessantly until picked up: but there is nothing wrong about wanting to be loved. Adults, too, need to be loved.

It is difficult for you, as a mother, when your baby is excessively demanding of your time. You have to get on with the housework. If you have another young child, you have to do things for him too and give him some of your time. A very demanding infant is difficult for you, but you just have to do your best to pick him up as much as reasonably possible, and you must not feel guilty if you cannot do it all the time. It certainly does no harm to leave him crying for short periods: but it is wrong to leave him crying for a long time during the day for fear of spoiling him. It is a different matter at night: if he has developed the habit of repeatedly crying out at night, that is a habit which has to be broken. Daytime demands for being picked up and loved soon decrease as he matures if his demands are met.

The older child, from 2 or so, thrives on love. As he gets older, and understands what is being said about him, you must be careful not to say things (jokingly) in front of him, which he may interpret as lack of love. It is always a mistake to threaten desertion, or deprivation of love, if a child does not do what he is told to do. He constantly wants to be loved, to feel wanted, to feel important: you must at all times avoid the weapons of ridicule, sarcasm, derogation, disparagement, and constant criticism or reprimands. In many homes almost the only conversation which the child hears is 'don't do this, don't do that', and threats of punishment if he disobeys. Particularly when he is older, he will be much disturbed if you constantly disapprove of what he says and does. He needs to be accepted and praised for good behaviour: praise for good behaviour is far more effective than criticism and blame for bad behaviour.

Children are upset by comparisons with their brother or sister. A mother may say to a boy that his sister would not do such a thing, or that she would do something she was asked to do, whereas he refuses. Such comparisons cause jealousy and insecurity. They are especially liable to occur if a parent shows favouritism. Nothing causes jealousy more quickly than favouritism. A parent does not realise that he is showing it, but it is obvious to everyone else. The parent who shows favouritism to a child is more tolerant towards him, he excuses his actions, he listens more to his stories, helps him more, plays with him more, and may give him more than he does to the other children. It makes the unfavoured feel unwanted and insecure. Children may rapidly (and often totally irrationally) feel that they are not wanted, not loved as much as a brother or sister, and they feel insecure as a result.

Insecurity is caused by friction at home — friction between the mother and father, or friction between parent and child. Friction between parent and child is easy to understand: parents are upset by the child's constant noisiness, crying, negativism, untidiness, selfishness, aggressiveness,

rudeness, lack of consideration for others, dawdling, carelessness over his clothes and appearance, bad behaviour in the
presence of visitors or strangers, untruthfulness, timidity,
lack of initiative — and many features of his behaviour which
the parent is unable to control, such as wetting and soiling
himself, tics, stuttering, constant activity, refusal to eat,
sleep or use the pottie. A child totally fails to recognise the
fact that his mother is tired, worried, hurried or unwell: and
as a result his mother responds by loss of her usual tolerance
and sense of humour, snaps at the child, punishes him and
makes him all the more insecure. Children need loving most
when they are most unloveable. Adolescents appreciate
tolerance, love and understanding most when they feel
irritable and bad tempered. Lasting love is made up of
hundreds of occasions when love and tolerance are shown.

A feeling of insecurity manifests itself in any of numerous
different ways — often entirely through the subconscious
mind, so that the real reason for the child's behaviour may for
a long time pass unrecognised. The signs of insecurity
include excessive quarrelsomeness, negativism, aggressiveness, temper tantrums, moodiness, rudeness, jealousy, fears,
nightmares, overactivity, attention seeking, lying, stealing,
delinquency, accident-proneness, wetting and soiling, nail
biting, thumb sucking, masturbation and tics. It is an important cause of underachievement, poor concentration and day-
dreaming. It is a factor in the cause of stuttering. Why some
children react in one way to insecurity, and others in another
way, we do not know.

Will it harm his development if I go to work?

Some mothers fear that their child will suffer emotionally if
they go out to work. Some feel guilty about working, while
leaving their child or children in charge of someone else, or, if
the mother is fortunate, in a creche or play group. The effect
on the children depends on the quality of care when she is at
work: if the quality is good, there is no evidence that the

children suffer in any way. If the quality is poor, or if the children get back to an empty home or have to wait outside for the mother's return, then they may suffer emotionally, and develop symptoms of insecurity. Children have to learn to accept separation from their mother, for they must acquire independence.

If a mother decides not to work outside the home, and to devote her entire time to her children (who themselves are a full time occupation) she may be entirely happy to do so: but others, especially those trained in some profession or skill, are liable to feel thwarted and bored, their temper suffers and this has a bad effect on the children. Furthermore, it is desirable for a mother to be trained in work which she could do if her husband became ill or died. On the other hand a mother of young children who is also at work probably has many more hours of work than her husband: she has responsibility of finding help to look after the children, the responsibility of dealing with their illnesses, and of shopping and running the home. She may come back tired and bad tempered, and so the children may suffer.

Much depends on her personality, energy and enjoyment of her work and the satisfaction which it gives her. She gains from acquiring self confidence, and from meeting others. As for the possible effect on her relationship with her husband, there is no evidence generally that her working does any harm at all.

Provided that the arrangements for the care of your children are satisfactory, and you find your work satisfying, there are no grounds for feeling guilty about leaving your children. It will do them no harm, and it may help them on the way to independence.

What about discipline?

Wise, loving discipline is essential for the emotional development of all children. They must learn at home to accept a 'No', to learn that they cannot have all that they want, to learn behaviour acceptable to others. They must learn that if they disobey something unpleasant will happen to them. This is important, for the child who is constantly being told not to do this, that, or the other, and who is not punished if he disobeys, will not learn to obey. This does not mean that there should be rigid discipline, frequent physical punishment or authoritarianism: all these are harmful. Children learn discipline far more by praise and encouragement for good behaviour than by reprimands and punishment for bad behaviour. They should learn to do what they are told to do because they want praise and love from their parents — not because they fear punishment if they disobey. Some parents are far too strict for fear of spoiling their child — and troublesome behaviour problems can result.

Attempts to teach discipline before the child is ready to learn are doomed to failure and lead to insecurity. Misjudgement of a child's developmental level is a common fault. One sees 10-month-old babies smacked for sucking the thumb: but they are far too young to learn cause and effect (and in any case there is nothing wrong about their sucking the thumb). Somewhere between 1 and 3 years of age the child begins to learn: this must depend in large part on his intelligence and therefore on his level of development: the bright 2-year-old can learn much more than a dull 4-year-old.

Much punishment can be avoided by wise management — for instance by distracting the child instead of punishing him. Constant reprimands and threats must always be avoided. Physical punishment is rarely necessary, and is never necessary for the older child after six or so. Before that age a single slap on the bottom is all that is needed: it is *never* necessary to hurt a child. If punishment is necessary, isolation or deprivation of something which the child likes is the best treatment.

Consistency is essential. The child cannot learn if one parent excuses what the other forbids, or if certain behaviour is allowed at one time and forbidden at another. You should not keep stopping your child from what he is doing unless there is a good reason, as in the case of dangerous practices, such as playing on the stairs. All too often children are reprimanded for actions which are in no way wrong. Again, you must not expect too much of your child in relation to his level of development. The wise parent makes no comment when the young child, learning to feed himself, uses his fingers rather than a spoon, knife or fork. You will cause friction between yourself and your children if you continually try to stop them doing things which are in no way wrong and which just do not matter. In many homes, each day is one long day of remonstrances over things which are not of the slightest importance: it is a potent cause of unhappiness and insecurity.

Lack of discipline makes a child insecure. It leads to bad behaviour, wailing and unhappiness: it presents difficulties for the child when he starts school and has to learn the hard way. It is a major cause of later delinquency and accident proneness. However, excessive discipline in many ways has a similar effect — insecurity, accident proneness, rebellion against authority and maybe delinquency.

Many parents have told me that they cannot understand their child's behaviour. They say that they have given him everything that money can buy: that if he wanted something he had only to ask to get it. But they do not realise that what he really wanted was something that money cannot buy — love, security and wise discipline.

How can I help him to become independent?

Children take pleasure in practising their newly acquired skills. They should be given every encouragement to use them as soon as they appear: they should be helped to learn independence in feeding themselves, dressing themselves, washing and so on. They should be given the responsibility of helping in the home, of going on simple errands, of doing shopping and so on as soon as they are ready. They need to learn what is safe and unsafe, to profit from experience, but not to be exposed to dangers until they are ready to face them. You have to take calculated risks — and strike a balance between these calculated risks and foolhardy carelessness and thoughtlessness about possible consequences of what one allows them to do or asks them to do. They must not be put into situations for which they are not ready.

Children have to learn to tolerate short absences from their mother. For this reason, amongst others, you should have short breaks away from your small child, provided that he will be well looked after. He must not be treated as a baby long after he has reached the age of largely looking after himself. He must be allowed freedom to make decisions — as long as they do not result in danger which he could not foresee: he should be allowed to participate in decisions which affect his life and future. Above all, he must gradually be allowed responsibility for his own life. Once more, however, you must not expect too much of him in relation to his intelligence, personality and stage of maturity.

It is a good thing to let a child stay a night or weekend with friends — as soon as you think that he is mature enough — and he should be allowed to have a friend staying with him in your home. Even if he does not stay a night or two with friends, it is good for him to visit the homes of his friends (without you, as soon as he is ready for it) and to have friends in your home.

Help your child to become independent by not being over-anxious and overprotective. You will hold him back if you do everything for him instead of letting him learn to do things for himself. Innumerable mothers feed their children long after properly managed children feed themselves without help. Innumerable mothers dress their children every morning, long after properly managed children dress themselves fully — apart, perhaps, from managing buttons at the back or tying shoe laces. Mothers argue that it is quicker to dress them than to let them do it themselves: it is, at first, but if allowed slowly to learn to do it themselves they will be fully independent long before other children — and so save much of their mother's time. When everything is done for a child who could perfectly well look after himself, it becomes unnecessary for him to make any effort.

When the child is at school, some parents help him with his homework, or do it for him, or check it when he has done it. If he complains about a teacher, they invariably support him without hearing the other side. Mothers say 'don't get your feet wet', 'don't catch cold' — and prevent him taking part in sport in case he might get hurt or catch something. They worry about his bowels; they call him 'delicate'; they keep him a baby instead of letting him grow up. Mothers obtain a certificate from the doctor for their child to be 'excused' from P.E. ('gym') or games, because they fear that it will be too rough for him. I know of a child who was not allowed to mix with other children in case he should pick up the local accent. Mothers are especially liable to overprotect their child if he has some handicap, such as asthma, which is natural but one must distinguish mother love from smother love.

This sort of overprotection is also liable to occur when the parents have had a long wait before conception, or when there is an only child, or a child is conceived accidentally long after the other children have grown up, or when the mother knows that she must not or cannot have another child. It occurs when there has been a bereavement, or when a child has recovered from a serious illness.

The result of overprotection is an immature personality. The child may be effeminate and timid, unable to defend himself; he may become unduly dependent on his mother, and unable to make decisions for himself; he is liable to be selfish and to find it difficult to establish satisfactory relationships with his peers. Some, on the other hand, rebel against authority, become aggressive and accident prone.

Help him to be a nice person

Some parents make the mistake of thinking that their child

will grow up to be perfect. When, in adolescence, his imperfections become obvious, they show their disapproval in no uncertain way. It is vital that children and adolescents should be accepted and loved, and that it should be fully recognised that no one is perfect. Parents are particularly liable to be irked by and to criticise those imperfections and undesirable traits of personality from which they suffer themselves. Nevertheless, good parents want their children to grow up to be nice happy people: and a person who is nice may well ultimately achieve much more in life than a person who is brilliant and extremely clever, but not so nice.

I suggest that if a child is to grow up to be a nice person, he should above all things learn to treat others as he would like to be treated: that means that he should be able to put himself into the position of the other; it means that he will avoid criticising others; that he will look for the good in people rather than the bad; that he will seek the charitable explanation of their actions; that he will be tolerant to the point of view of others. He will recognise that there may be two sides to a question, two points of view, and that either or both may be right. He will be tolerant to others who may not be as clever as he, or who learn more slowly, or who have different aptitudes. He will never knowingly be unkind to others, he will not be a bully, or tell tales. He will accept defeat in games or arguments gracefully — as a good loser. He will not cheat, he will learn to give and take, he will mix and cooperate equally with people no matter what social class, race, colour, sex, religion or opinion. He will not boast, show off or gloat over the deficiencies of others. He will take the lead, as occasion arises, but will not insist on leading. He will learn independence of thought and action. He has freedom to be different — in dress, thought and action, and will tolerate nonconformity in others, but he will learn the difference between right and wrong, and so must learn good moral values. He will not be led astray by friends or gangs into actions which are unkind. He will develop a sensible attitude to sex; and he will be sensible about illness — not exaggerating the symptoms but taking it in his stride. Above all, he will learn to treat others as he would like to be treated himself.

When should I ask the doctor's advice?

It is difficult to make a precise statement about this. I have tried in this chapter to emphasize that most of the troublesome behaviour of small children is normal and that they will outgrow it. But if you are still worried, seek advice from your family doctor.

3. HOW SHOULD HE DEVELOP PHYSICALLY ?

As in all other aspects of development, there is a big difference between the *average* and the *normal*. A child may be pounds below the average in weight, or inches below the average in height, and yet be normal. All one can say is that the further away from the average a child is in anything, the more likely it is that there is some cause, perhaps disease. In the section to follow I shall give *average* figures for various ages from birth onwards, but I shall make no attempt to give the range of normal, for that is always impossible.

Birth weight

A baby's weight at birth depends upon a wide variety of factors. What and how much you eat during pregnancy — particularly in the last three months — will affect your baby's weight at birth. He is likely to be large if you gain a great deal of weight during your pregnancy or if you are fairly tall and heavy anyway. He is also likely to be large if you have diabetes; and if you are over 24 each baby you have is likely to be heavier than the last. It is said that the largest live-born baby weighed 20 lbs 8 oz!

Your baby will almost certainly be born lighter in weight than the average if your pregnancy does not last more than 37 weeks. From Table 1 you can see how heavy he is likely to be.

Table 1

Weeks of pregnancy	1bs (kg)
28	2.9 (1.3)
30	3.6 (1.6)
32	4.2 (1.9)
34	5.2 (2.4)
36	6.4 (2.9)
38	6.9 (3.1)
40	7.5 (3.4)

Your baby is likely to be born smaller if your pregnancy has continued for too long, if you have had certain infections during pregnancy, if you are having twins or if you smoke, drink or take other drugs in excess.

Apart from all this, there may simply be a tendency in your family to have large or small babies.

Growth after birth

You should have your baby weighed regularly, particularly if you are breast-feeding him so that you can be certain he is getting enough milk. It is reasonable to weigh him once a week for the first two months, once a month for the rest of his first year, and then about once every six months. But do not weigh him more often as you will only become worried when his weight gain temporarily slows down because of a cold or some other unimportant infection. In the first three months after birth the average weight gain is 7 oz a week (196.g), in the second three months 5.3 oz (148.g) a week, in the third three months 3½ oz (113.g) a week, and in the last three months 2½ oz (71.g) a week. In the second year the average child gains only about 1½ oz (42.g) per week. So do not worry when your child stops gaining weight so quickly and perhaps wants less to eat. It is perfectly normal, and it does not mean that he is unwell. Even when a child has had an illness, such as an infection, he will go through 'catch-up growth' — a period of increased appetite and more rapid weight gain until he has made up lost ground.

25

A child who is small at birth, especially if he were small in relation to the duration of pregnancy, is usually smaller than average in later years: and the bigger the baby at birth the bigger is he usually later. There are other factors, especially the weight and build of the parents. I have seen scores of mothers (and nurses and doctors) concerned about a child's small size, because they have failed to realise that he was small at birth — and that his mother is small in height and build. I have seen a mother accused of starving her child who was far below the average weight; but he was 4½ lbs at full-term birth, and his mother weighed 7 stones and was 4 feet 11 inches tall. A confusing fact is that a baby's weight at birth may be average or even above average, when a mother is unusually small, and then his weight gain may be slower than average, which raises fears that there is something wrong. Apart from this, there is often an inherited pattern of growth, so that the growth in weight and height may be unusually slow in the early months, the child catching up to the average as he gets older. There is some evidence that children who had a very low birth weight are more often than others smaller than usual even after puberty, but of course there are exceptions.

Unusual tallness is usually a family trait: but most fat children are also tall for their age.

The average weight and height in the first five years is shown in Table 2.

Expected adult height

If your child is unusually small or tall, you may like to know what height the child is likely to reach as an adult. Table 3 shows the height which an adult of 5 feet, 5 feet 6 inches or 6 feet would probably have reached at various ages in the first five years. At the second birthday a child has reached very nearly half the eventual height.

For example, a 2-year-old boy who is 32.1 inches in length, is likely to be about 5' 6" as an adult. A girl who is 33.9 inches

Table 2. Weight and height from birth to 5 years

Age	Weight		Height	
	Pounds	kg	Inches	cm
GIRLS				
Birth	7.5	3.4	20.9	53.0
3 months	12.3	5.6	—	—
6 months	15.2	6.9	—	—
9 months	19.2	8.7	—	—
1 year	21.4	9.7	29.2	74.2
2 years	26.9	12.2	33.7	85.6
3 years	31.5	14.3	36.6	93.0
4 years	35.9	16.3	39.5	100.4
5 years	40.3	18.3	42.4	107.2
BOYS				
Birth	7.7	3.5	21.3	54.0
3 months	13.1	5.9	—	—
6 months	17.4	7.9	—	—
9 months	20.3	9.2	—	—
1 year	22.5	10.2	30.0	76.3
2 years	28.0	12.7	34.2	86.9
3 years	32.4	14.7	37.1	94.2
4 years	36.6	16.6	40.0	101.6
5 years	40.7	18.5	42.6	108.3

Table 3. Height in childhood in relation to expected adult height

		Expected adult height				
	5'	150 cm	5'6''	165 cm	6'	180
Boys	Age in years					
	1	25.8	65.5	28.3	72.0	30.9	78.6
	2	29.4	74.7	32.1	81.7	35.3	89.6
	3	31.8	80.8	35.1	89.2	38.1	97.0
	4	34.4	87.3	37.8	96.1	41.2	104.7
	5	36.6	93.0	40.3	102.3	43.9	111.6
Girls	1	27.0	68.5	28.3	72.0	32.4	81.0
	2	31.1	79.2	34.3	87.1	37.4	95.0
	3	33.9	86.0	37.2	94.5	40.6	103.1
	4	36.5	92.8	40.2	102.1	43.9	111.4
	5	39.0	99.1	43.0	109.1	46.9	119.0

long at the age of 3 is likely to reach an adult height of about 5 feet.

Why is he not growing properly?

Your child's growth may differ from the average not only because of his weight when he was born and family tendencies, but also because of the food he eats. If he does not have enough nourishing food he will not grow properly. Another reason for some children not thriving is that they are deprived of love and affection and may even be rejected by their parents. This can hold back their physical development considerably.

If you are worried about your child's weight or height, you should first of all consider these possibilities. If none of them seem to apply, and yet the child if full of energy, and is apparently well and happy, it is unlikely that there is any disease. But many things, such as not absorbing all the food that is eaten, may hold back growth, and if in doubt, you should consult your doctor. You should certainly consult him if the child seems unwell. More important than a single measurement of weight is a series of measurements: a child health clinic would plot the child's weight on a chart, and if there is any falling off in weight gain (apart from the normal falling off in the first year, mentioned above), the doctor should be consulted. Remember that scales may be inaccurate: if you weigh the child on different scales there may be considerable differences in the weight recorded.

But remember that there is nothing to be said for the idea that the bigger a child is, the better he is. It is much more healthy to be below the average weight than above it. *It is far more important that the child should be well and full of energy, than that he should be average in weight.*

Why is he getting fat?

The answer is that although we know many of the causes of

overweight, there is much that we do not know or understand. Basically no one can get fat unless he eats more than he needs. The main causes of obesity are therefore eating too much, or lack of exercise. But that is a gross oversimplification. Many children and adults have an enormous appetite and eat accordingly, but remain thin: others become fat on an intake of food which is in no way excessive. There are undoubtedly genetic or hereditary factors: where both parents are an average weight, only one child in 10 will be overweight. When one parent is overweight, there is a 40 per cent likelihood that the children will be too: and when both parents are overweight, there is an 80 per cent likelihood that the children will be overweight. But the fact that 2 or 3 members of a family are overweight does not prove a hereditary factor. The family may simply like good food and plenty of it. Do not be tempted to think there 'must be something wrong with his glands' when your child is fat. In fact it is most unusual that the doctor can prove that there is anything wrong in this way.

Why do some children eat more than they need?

There are many possible reasons. Sometimes a mother regards her child as delicate because he was an unusually small, perhaps premature, baby, or because he had some illness, and she is then determined to 'build up his strength'. Habit is important: the amount of potatoes or toast which we eat is governed more by habit than by hunger. Jealousy may be a factor: when a girl sees her brother ask for another helping of pudding, she asks for more herself, partly so that she cannot be outdone by him and partly so that he cannot have it all. But the most obvious example of the importance of habit is eating sweets. This is a most unfortunate habit started by the parents. Sweets are costly, damaging to the teeth, fattening, and often spoil the child's appetite for proper meals. Parents give children sweets because they think that this is a good way of showing love or giving reward. Almost invariably when one gives an older child an injection for immunisation, the mother gives him a sweet. The first thing that many adults do when they sit down in a cinema or concert is eat sweets. Children also eat sweets because they see their parents eat them. Nearly all fat children are constantly eating sweets, potato crisps or salted nuts, and are having constant snacks between meals. Mothers say that their boy is 'such a big fellow, he needs a lot to fill him': but he has become a big fellow because of overeating. Most fat children are tall for their age. Many mothers have the totally wrong idea that the bigger the baby or child is the better, and they refer to their fat, ugly child as 'bonny'. Obesity is much more a problem of the lower social classes than the middle and upper ones: this may be partly due to unwise choice of food in the lower classes. Some people think that feeding a baby cereal at an early age may cause overweight.

Children, like adults, often eat food when they are feeling insecure, worried, bored or waiting for something to happen.

It is far easier to prevent obesity than to treat it once it has developed. When a young baby demands larger than usual feeds, it can be very difficult to ignore his demands. Excessive weight gain as early as six weeks of age makes it more likely that the child will be overweight later. Nevertheless, many children who are overweight at 12 months thin out as they grow — but nevertheless, they are more likely than others to be overweight in later years. One can certainly avoid starting the sweet-eating habit. Weight measurements taken regularly are of great importance, for they soon show whether a child's weight gain is excessive or not. If it is excessive, the food intake must be cut down: your doctor will advise you.

The worst foods for the overweight person are sweets, chocolate, peanut butter, peanuts, potato crisps, butter, margarine, cream cheese, cheese straws and bacon: other fattening foods are sugar, ice cream, jam, honey, tinned fruit, cakes, pudding, macaroni, biscuits, cornflakes, cheese (except cottage cheese), fried foods, sausage and sausage roll and bottled fruit drinks. Meat, fruit, vegetables, baked beans and fish are much less likely to cause obesity.

Is his head too big?

Mothers, doctors and nurses are sometimes anxious because a baby's head is smaller or bigger than usual. There are some important conditions, which must be diagnosed promptly, because they can be treated, so if in doubt you must consult your doctor. But remember that a big baby is obviously likely to have a bigger head than a small baby, and a small baby a smaller head than a big baby. In addition, if a parent has an unusually small or large head, his children may take after him.

Table 4 shows the average head circumference in the first year — only for children of average weight.

Table 4

Age	Inches	cm
Birth	14	35
3 months	15.8	39.5
6 months	17.0	42.5
9 months	17.8	44.5
12 months	18.2	45.5

The shape of a baby's head may cause anxiety. The head is commonly flat on one side, with a corresponding bulge at the other side: this is normal, and is nearly always due to the baby preferring to lie on one side. The peculiarity disappears after a few months. Other peculiarities of the shape, such as a bulging forehead, are commonly a familial feature.

The top of the baby's head has a soft area which is usually small at birth and enlarges during the first two or more months, after which it becomes smaller and closes. Usually it closes by 12 to 18 months, but it may close in normal children much sooner — say 3 or 4 months — or much later.

The teeth

Approximately one in every thousand children is born with a tooth, but the average age at which the first tooth appears is 6 months — usually a bottom front tooth. The top front teeth usually appear about a month later. There are usually 6 teeth at the age of 1 year, and the first set of 20 teeth is usually complete by 2½ years. The first tooth of the second set does not usually appear till 5 or 6 years of age. Some children are much later than the average in teething, so if your child's teeth have not appeared by 12 months or so it does not mean that anything is wrong. The age of teething commonly runs in the family. When a child is born with a tooth, there is no need to extract it.

Teething does *not* cause bronchitis, rashes, convulsions, fever or diarrhoea. But it may cause dribbling, and *occasionally* food refusal. It does not cause crying at night.

Care of the teeth

The *care* of the teeth begins when the first tooth has completely erupted, when it is gently brushed morning and evening. This is sometimes easier said than done. But by the age of three, the child should brush his own teeth, at first under supervision.

You can help to prevent your child's teeth decaying by (1) using a toothpaste which contains fluoride; and if your water supply also contains fluoride this will halve the chances of his teeth decaying. (2) Do not give him sweets between meals, and be careful not to give him too many other sweet things. Fruit syrup and squash damages teeth; and you should never give your baby a dummy or pacifier coated with honey, syrup or glycerine. (3) If your child's teeth are overcrowded after the age of about 5, food can become stuck between them and cause decay, so you should see your dentist about this.

It is a shame to let a child's appearance be spoiled by prominent front teeth, so if his second teeth come through this way you should have this corrected.

Prevention of infection

It is important for your child to be immunised against certain infections (e.g. whooping cough, polio), so discuss this with your doctor.

Some features of physical development which cause anxiety

Tongue tie

It would be an exaggeration to say that significant tongue tie never occurs, but it is true to say that it is very rare. I have never seen a case which required surgical treatment. The fold of flesh under the tongue of the young baby suggests that there is 'tongue tie': in fact the tip of the tongue nearly always grows forward as the months go by. 'Tongue tie' does not interfere with speech.

Alveolar frenum

The alveolar frenum is the fold of flesh under the middle of the upper lip. It does not usually require treatment, but occasionally it separates the two top front teeth, and surgical treatment is then required.

Watering of the eyes

Normally the tear duct carries the tears from the eyes to the nose. Frequently the duct does not open fully for several weeks, and the eyes then water. The duct almost always opens up in time and you should not expect your doctor to do anything about it, at least in the first 6 to 12 months.

Squint

If there is a fixed squint, it should be treated, whatever the age. Normally, however, if there is a squint it is not there all the time. After your child is about 6 months old it is most important that a squint should be treated, for if left much after the first year he will become blind in the squinting eye. If in doubt — as mothers and doctors (including paediatricians) often are, arrange for your child to be seen by an eye specialist — and do not delay.

Hernias

If you notice a bulge where the baby's navel is, this is nothing to worry about and no treatment is required. You should not put on strapping, buttons, coins or anything else. Nearly all hernias of this type cure themselves by the time the child is 4 or 5 years old.

However, if there is a bulge in the baby's groin you must take him to the doctor, for unless this is treated promptly he may become seriously ill. The younger the child is when it is found, the more important it is to have it treated.

Hydrocele

This is a collection of fluid in the scrotum (the pouch containing the testes, or testicles). It usually cures itself in a few months, so that no treatment is needed, certainly in the first year.

Undescended testes

Occasionally the testes have not descended into the scrotum but are up inside the body. Your doctor will be able to advise you if you think this might be the case. When this happens it is important that the child should be operated on, normally between 2 and 4 years of age, but not later.

The foreskin

In the vast majority of boys circumcision is totally unnecessary. The foreskin can only rarely be retracted (pulled back) in the early months, but it will retract in two or three years or so. Leave it alone. Even if the foreskin appears to be 'long', or 'bent', or to 'balloon out when the boy passes urine', do nothing about it. It is only when a foreskin has been so scarred by a neglected nappy rash that it can never be retracted is circumcision necessary.

Bow legs

All babies appear to have bow legs. Provided that both are bowed, and the bowing is not excessive, nothing is done, for they are normal. If in doubt, consult your doctor.

Knock knee

Almost all toddlers appear to have knock knees. Provided that both legs are the same, almost all cure themselves. If there is significant knock knee after about five years of age, consult your doctor.

Toeing in (or out)

Very many children when they first start walking turn their toes in. Provided that it is the same on both sides, nothing is done about it: it rights itself. If there is marked turning in or out by the age of 6 years, ask your family doctor to refer you to an orthopaedic specialist with experience of children.

Flat feet

Young children appear to have flat feet because of the pad of fat in the sole of the foot. It is normal.

Curly toes

When toes overlap, one does nothing unless there is actual

soreness, and then at the age of three or four years an ortho-paedic surgeon should see the child, and an operation may be done. Strapping is useless.

Donkey ears

If a child's ears stick out it can cause him embarrassment. A surgeon will correct this after the age of 6 or so.

4. HOW SHOULD HE DEVELOP MENTALLY?

Introduction

Here I shall outline the normal development of the child apart from his physical and emotional development and give the average age at which he might be able to do various things. But do please note that *there is a vast difference between the average and the normal*. Just because for example, your child starts walking later than the child next door, this does not mean that there is anything wrong with your baby. All children are different, and they differ in all aspects of development, mental, physical and emotional. Very few children are average in all fields of development: some normal children are able to do some things earlier than others who have the same level of intelligence, and some later than others who are no more intelligent. It is a serious mistake — and one which doctors often make — to say that a child *should* be able to do such-and-such a thing by a certain age. It is impossible to draw the line between normal and abnormal, so the best one can do is talk about the average age at which children do things.

I have mentioned below numerous features of the child's development, numerous milestones and numerous things which you can look out for. But the list is by no means complete: you will notice a great deal more in your own child if you watch his development.

Different patterns of development

Your child's development may follow many different patterns — for example, he may be:

1. Average in all aspects of development and remaining so as he gets older. This must be rare.
2. Average in all fields in the early months, and later proving to be mentally superior. Perhaps the explanation of this would be the fact that our assessment in the early months failed to pick up the early indications of mental superiority.
3. Advanced in certain fields only. The significance of this depends on which fields the child excels in. If he is advanced, say, in sitting and walking it signifies nothing about his intelligence. But unusually advanced speech is an important indication of high intelligence.
4. Average or advanced in the early months, followed by slowing down in development as the months or years go by. The explanation sometimes lies in unsatisfactory home environment.
5. The slow starter — backwardness in all fields in the early months followed by average intelligence or mental superiority later. This undoubtedly occurs, but it is rare.
6. Retarded in some fields, average or advanced in others. This is very common; often it runs in the family.
7. Retarded in all, remaining below average. This is the usual picture of a lower than average level of intelligence.
8. Lulls in development. These are common. It is particularly common to see a child who when learning to walk makes apparently no progress in the development of speech for some weeks: and then suddenly speech makes startling progress. I have seen children who were considerably retarded in speech in one month and unusually advanced in speech next month.

As you watch your baby develop you should bear one or two basic points in mind. No child can do anything until his nervous system is ready for it. When he is born his nervous system is simply not developed enough to enable him to walk, for instance, but as soon as he shows signs of being ready to do anything you should let him practice as much as possible. He will enjoy it too.

The sequence of development is the same in all children, but the speed of development varies widely. For example, all children sit before they walk, but the age at which they can do these things varies from child to child.

The direction of development is from the head downwards. Children understand much before they use their hands and they use their hands long before they walk.

As he grows older your baby will gain greater control of his body. At six months his whole body and all his limbs will move in excitement and interest over some fascinating toy. A few months later he will simply smile and reach out for it without kicking his legs.

A baby's development is continuous from the time he is conceived and birth is simply an event during the course of development. If your baby is premature it therefore stands to reason that he may not be as far developed as another baby of the same 'age' who was not born prematurely.

General factors which affect development

The way and speed at which your child will develop depends on many factors. One of these is the rate of maturing of the nervous system, mentioned above, which is often something which runs in families. Often several people in one family walk, or become dry, or start to speak notably late or early, although they are of average intelligence.

The sex of your child also plays a part: on average girls walk, talk and become dry earlier than boys.

The personality of the child has some bearing on his development: for instance, some babies are much more cautious than others when learning to stand or walk, and are more afraid of falling or are more put off by a fall than are other more daring characters.

The child's level of intelligence (which is partly inherited and partly influenced by home and surroundings) has a profound effect on his development. The mentally subnormal child is late in all aspects of development (except occasionally sitting and walking): in addition he shows less interest in his surroundings, is less responsive, less alert, and has a poor span of attention, concentrating badly: whereas the mentally gifted child has the opposite — good attention span, good concentration, more interest in surroundings — but is not necessarily advanced in the age of walking and sitting. Usually the gifted child is advanced as a baby in the use of his hands, and the dull child retarded in it. It seems that there is some connection between the level of in-born intelligence and the level of maturity of the nervous system at birth: for instance, the dull child is always late in beginning to smile at the mother in response to her overtures, and the bright child often begins to smile unusually early.

Table 5 shows the range of intelligence quotient scores in children.

Table 5. IQ scores in children

IQ scores	Percentage of children	IQ scores	Proportion of children
150 or more	0.1		
130—149	1.0	over 180	1 in 1 million
120—129	5.0	over 170	1 in 100 000
110—119	14.0	over 160	1 in 10 000
100—109	30.0	over 150	1 in 1000
90—99	30.0	over 140	1 in 170
80—89	14.0	over 136	1 in 100
70—79	5.0	over 125	1 in 17
Below 70	1.0		

You can greatly affect your child's development by the way in which you treat him. For instance, he will be held back in developing the ability to feed himself, dress himself and attend to his toilet needs, if you do not give him a chance to practise and learn. (see page 4).

Many physical conditions delay development in various fields. For instance, a defect of hearing will delay the development of speech. Floppiness (reduced muscle tone) delays sitting and walking; stiffness (spasticity, cerebral palsy) greatly delays development of sitting, walking and the use of the hands: and chronic illness may retard development in general.

The preterm baby

The definition of a preterm (premature) baby is one born from a pregnancy of less than 37 weeks: and the definition of a low birth weight baby is one who at birth weighed 5½ lbs (2500 g) or less.

By examination of the baby one can determine to within a week the duration of the pregnancy. This can be important, because you may not always be sure of your dates. One assesses the baby by physical and neurological features: the physical features include the skin texture and colour, the form and firmness of the ears, the breast size and nipple formation, and the descent of the testes into the scrotum. The neurological features include the posture when lying on the back, how far the wrist and foot can be flexed; the degree of extension of the knee when the hip is fully flexed, and the 'scarf' sign — whereby one carries the baby's hand in front of his neck to his shoulder: a baby born at 32 weeks gets his hand well beyond the tip of the shoulder (and when one rotates the head, he can also get the chin well beyond the tip of the shoulder), while the full-term (not premature) baby can only get the hand or chin as far as the shoulder tip.

When a baby is born prematurely, he is naturally less developed than one which is not premature. Hence one must allow for this in assessing his development in the coming weeks. For instance, if he is born 2 months early, he will be expected, if average, to begin to smile at his mother not at 4 to 6 weeks, the usual time for a full-term baby, but at 4 to 6 weeks plus 2 months: and instead of expecting him to sit for a

41

few seconds on the floor without support at 7 months, one expects him to do it at 7 + 2 months = 9 months. This does not imply that he is 'backward': it is a matter of common sense that if he is born 2 months early, he must only be compared subsequently with the average performance of full term babies by adding 2 months to the age at which they acquire certain skills. Obviously as he gets older the difference of two months makes less and less difference and then can be ignored.

The newborn full- term baby — the first four weeks

The full-term newborn baby is not just a reflex being who cries, drinks and wets. He is born with a remarkable range of abilities and degree of awareness. He can focus with his eyes and will follow with his eyes over an arc of 90° or more. He looks longer at a black or white drawing of a face than he will at three black dots on a white card:. He shows more interest in a black and white pattern than a blank grey card:. He responds more to a proper picture of a face than to a picture with the eyes, nose, mouth, ears etc. mixed up in the wrong position. By 2 weeks he can distinguish his mother's face from that of strangers and watches his mother's face longer. He reacts more to his mother's face when she is talking to him than when her face is expressionless. By 3 weeks he reacts differently to persons and objects. He adjusts to distance: when an object moves towards his face, he pulls his head back. It is said that at 3 or 4 weeks he fixes his eyes more on the edge of a face than on other parts, but at 7 weeks he looks more at his mother's eyes, especially when she is talking to him. Psychologists claim that at 4 weeks he shows a rudimentary judgement of the size of two objects when shown them at different distances from his eyes.

On the first day he responds to sound. He begins to localise sound and in the first week to turn his head slightly to sound. Rhythmical or low frequency sounds tend to soothe him, while other sounds may make him cry, startle or blink. He can discriminate the intensity and duration of sound. He is said to respond more to a female voice than to a male one. His face alerts as he searches for the source of sound.

He has taste sense in the newborn period and responds differently to different tastes. A sugar coated finger causes him to suck and lick, and he follows the finger when it is withdrawn; a salt-coated finger makes him grimace, there is little sucking, and he does not follow it when it is withdrawn.

Within 6 to 10 days he responds to smell by turning to his mother's breast. He roots for milk when near the breast even if the breast is clothed. He localises smell and turns his head away from unpleasant smells. Within a week he shows preference for his mother's smell (as for her voice and face), as compared with that of strangers.

In these and other ways he begins to show understanding. It has been shown that when he is picked up, his visual alertness and interest in surroundings is increased. In the first month he begins to imitate tongue protrusion. It is said that a breast fed baby responds earlier than does an artificially fed baby.

Numerous mothers of a second or subsequent child have told me that in the first two or three days they have no doubt about the baby's personality and behaviour being different from that of the previous child.

You will probably find it difficult to confirm some of these observations, mainly made by psychologists, but you will find it interesting and stimulating to study and watch some of these early responses in your baby.

Reflexes of the newborn

There are very many 'reflexes' which can be readily demonstrated: they are involuntary actions, often depending on posture. For instance, if you pull the baby half up to the sitting position, and suddenly let him fall back an inch or two, his arms will come out from the body, the hands open, and the arms come together again (the Moro reflex). When you make a sudden noise, he blinks, startles and catches his breath: if crying he may momentarily stop, or if quiet he may cry. If you slip your finger into the palm of the hand, he will close on it: if you slip your finger across the sole of the foot, the toes flex. If you touch the corner of his mouth, the bottom lip is lowered on the same side, the tongue moving towards the point of stimulation. When the finger is moved away, the head turns to follow it. If you touch the centre of the upper lip, the lip elevates and the tongue moves towards it. If you hold him up so that his foot is pressed against a firm surface, and you gently push his head back, he will make walking movements. If you hold him up face down with your hand under the abdomen, and tickle gently the side of the body, he will bend sideways towards the stimulus.

All these reflexes disappear as the baby gets older.

The development of communication

Children communicate not just by speech, but by crying, smiling, laughing, playing, clinging, kissing, pushing a person away, or by the expression on the face. The young baby watches the mother intently long before the smile begins. The child responds to his mother, and the mother to her child: if the child responds, the mother responds and vice versa. She responds by the expression on her face, by talking to him, by the tone of her voice and by playing with him.

All children cry before they learn to smile. It is not always possible to determine why a baby cries. The common causes are the desire to be picked up, hunger, thirst, pain, fear, a change in posture, a loud noise, an unpleasant smell or taste, irritation by a rash, discomfort by cold or heat or a wet nappy, the passing of urine or a stool. Evening colic is a feature of some well thriving babies in their first three months — rhythmical screaming attacks mostly between 6.0 pm and 10.0 pm (easily prevented by the medicine dicyclomine hydrocloride — Merbentyl). Some cry when the light is put out, some when it is put on. One cannot please all of them. Many cry when the head or limbs are held. The quality of the cry often indicates the cause: the cry of pain or hunger is quite different from the cry of loneliness or fatigue. The amount of crying depends on the causes, and his personality, tolerance of discomfort, and his mother's responsiveness. We showed in the Jessop Obstetric Hospital in Sheffield that mothers can pick out the crying of their own baby as distinct from that of others within 48 hours of delivery.

As the child gets older, other causes of crying are found. Babies cry when they are tired, bored, when the mother or brother leaves the room or removes a toy, or when they are not allowed to help to feed themselves or to use a favourite cup: they develop likes and dislikes of food: they cry because of feelings of jealousy, they cry when being washed, or when the nose is cleaned. After about 6 months a sudden shriek at night could be a nightmare: but crying in the evening or night is more likely to be the result of habit formation, so that he learns that as soon as he cries he will be taken downstairs or into his mother's bed. At 6 months or so he may cry when a stranger speaks to him.

Before the smile begins, the baby watches his mother intently as she speaks to him, opening and closing his mouth, bobbing his head up and down, and often splaying out the toes. The first smile is usually around 4 to 6 weeks of age. I have seen the first smile much earlier — at 3 or 4 days of age. It is remarkable that there are still mothers who wonder if the baby's smile is due to 'wind': but I have never been able to understand why it should be thought that abdominal pain should make a child smile. The first smile is always in response to the mother's overtures. A week or two later the child begins to make cooing noises, as well as smiling. The first sounds are vowel sounds — ah, uh, eh. At 8 or 9 weeks the child may smile when he hears his mother's voice, before seeing her.

By 2 or 3 months he begins to add the letter g — as ga to his cooing. At 3 or 4 months he holds a long 'conversation' as his mother talks to him: and at about 4 months he squeals with pleasure, says 'Ah goo', begins to add the letters m, k, b and p and blows raspberries, enjoying the vibration in his lips. He laughs aloud. He soon adds ma, ba, ka, da, and at 7 months combines syllables to say mumum, dada — but not meaning mummy or daddy. He 'talks' to his toys, and his intonations become much more varied, with high and low pitch sounds. At 6 months he often laughs at the incongruous — when his father puts on a funny hat, or when a sister or brother amuses him. At about 10 months the factor of imitation begins — so that he begins to say words with meaning: but often he only says part of a word (e.g. 'g' or 'og' for 'dog') and soon imitates the noise made by dogs, cats, clocks etc, and responds to his own name.

Three out of four children say one word with meaning by the age of 12 months. At this age (12 months) the child develops jargon — expressive sounds which probably no one can understand, but with the odd clear word intermingled with it: and observation will show that his jargon is specific for certain meanings which he is trying to express. Soon the jargon disappears. By the age of 21 to 24 months the average child begins to join 2 or 3 words together (spontaneously, not just in imitation) and uses the words I, me and you. Indistinctness of speech is usual in the second and third year: the commonest form is the lisp, due to protrusion of the tongue between teeth on saying an 'S'. At three or so it is very common for the child when excited to appear to stutter — repeating syllables, but provided that no attempt is made to stop it, the 'stutter' *nearly* always cures itself — as does the lisp.

There are wide variations in the development of speech in normal children. Some bright babies say several words with meaning by 8 or 9 months: other bright children may say virtually no words till two or three years. Some exceptionally bright children join words together by 10 months or so, while others do not do this till nearly 4. One in 10 children has scarcely intelligible speech at 4. Unusual lateness in speech commonly runs in families.

Speech develops earlier, on the average, in girls and in the firstborn (perhaps largely because the mother has more time to talk to the firstborn than to subsequent children). All children learn the meaning of words long before they can say them. Naturally if a mother does not talk to her child much, speech development is delayed. Children learn speech more from their parents than from their brothers and sisters (or from play groups). Twins are often late in learning to talk, probably largely (but not entirely) because the mother has less time to talk to twins and read to them. The common lull in the development of speech when a child is learning other skills must be remembered.

Deafness inevitably delays speech. A child may have only high tone deafness, and can hear a car passing, a door banging, an aeroplane, or foot steps, and may respond to a low frequency whisper and so the parents do not realise that he is deaf: he cannot say the letters s and f, which are high tone sounds. The slightly deaf child can say the letters b, f, w, which he can see made, but not g, l and r. *If you are in doubt as to whether he can hear normally, you must have his hearing checked by an expert.* It is an invariable rule amongst paediatricians that the hearing must be checked by an expert whenever there is delay in speech development, or unusual indistinctness of speech.

An important factor in speech development is the child's level of intelligence. If this is below average, speech is delayed: but remember that speech may be delayed in brilliant children (as it was in the case of Albert Einstein). There is an ill-understood connection between the development of speech and the establishment of right or left handedness. Children with cerebral palsy are usually late in learning to talk.

Delayed speech is *not* due to tongue tie. It is *not* due to laziness: children do not speak because they cannot speak. It is *not* due to jealousy. It is *not* due to 'everything being done for him so that he does not try to speak'. Efforts to make a child

47

speak may cause serious behaviour problems and insecurity.

Stuttering, which is the same as stammering, is a complex problem. It usually starts between 2 and 4 years, and it is more common in boys. It may be the case that the child is imitating someone else who stutters. It may be due to the parents trying to make him speak distinctly, telling him to take a big breath before he speaks, to say it again, so making him selfconscious about his speech and causing a true stutter. Four out of five children with a mild stutter cure themselves: but if it should be marked, it should be treated by the fourth birthday. A speech therapist is likely to use the method of 'timed syllabic speech' — teaching the child to separate all syllables equidistantly.

Muscle control

Sitting and walking

The earliest sign of muscle control is the development of head control — which is dependent on the neck muscles. When you place the new baby face downwards on the floor he tends to draw his knees up under his abdomen: but by about six weeks he lies flat (except when asleep), and when awake he can momentarily lift his chin off the couch. If you hold him with your hand under his abdomen he momentarily holds his head up in the same plane as the body; but by 12 weeks he holds his head up well beyond the plane of his trunk. By 16 weeks when placed on his abdomen he can lift his chin and chest off the couch, when he feels like it: at 5 months he bears his weight on his forearms and can roll from front to back: a month later he bears his weight on his hands, and can roll from his back to his abdomen. At 6 months he sits on a firm surface with his hands forward on the couch for support: a month later he sits on the floor for a few seconds without rolling over. He characteristically bounces up and down when held in the standing position; and at 6 months when lying on his back on the floor he lifts his head up. By 8 months he can sit securely on the floor, and can stand holding on to furniture, and a month later he can pull himself up to the sitting position from lying on his abdomen. At 9 months when on his abdomen he may pull himself forward (crawling), or progress backwards unintentionally. A month later he crawls on hands and knees. At 11 months he walks, two hands held, or holding on to the furniture; at 12 months he walks with one hand held, and at 13 months manages a few steps without help although his steps are in varying directions and of varying length. He can sit down in a chair. At 15 months he creeps up stairs and can get into the standing position without help. He can also kneel. He cannot go round corners or stop suddenly. At 18 months he can get up and down stairs without help, and jumps with both feet. At 24 months he can pick an object up from the floor without falling and can run. At 3 years he can stand for a few seconds on one foot, and can go upstairs, one foot per step, and downstairs, two feet per step: and he can ride a tricycle. At 4 years he gets down stairs with one foot per step, and can hop on one foot.

Babies after about 9 months can progress in less orthodox ways than mere crawling or walking. Some progress by rolling; some lie on their back, lift their bottom, and progress with a series of bumps; some crawl backwards, and many progress rapidly by 'shuffling' or 'hitching' on one buttock and one hand.

As in all other fields of development, there are wide variations in motor development. Though the average age at which children first walk without help is 13 months, three per cent walk unaided by 9 months. I saw a child actively creeping on hands and knees at 4½ months, walking when holding on to furniture at 6 months, and walking without help at 8 months; but he was in no way a clever boy, and was in fact backward and below average in his school work, with an IQ score of 88.

Most, but not all, mentally backward children are later than average in walking: but I have seen many normal children who could not walk without help until after the second birthday. The age of sitting and walking — early or late — is commonly a hereditary feature. A floppy baby or a spastic baby is late in walking. I have already mentioned the effect of personality on the age of walking, with its effect on the child's confidence. Some children are held back by not being given a chance to bear weight on the legs, because the mother fears that standing will cause rickets, knock-knee or bow legs. A blind child may be late in walking. Obesity or congenital dislocation of the hip does not delay walking.

The use of the hands

I have mentioned the grasp reflex, whereby when one slides one's finger across the palm of the hand or sole of the foot, the baby closes on it: this reflex is lost after 2 or 3 months, by which time you may also observe that the hands tend to be open much more than when he was younger. At about three months he will hold a rattle placed in the hand and play with it, but if he drops it he cannot pick it up, neither can he reach out and get an object unless it is placed in his hand — though you can see that he looks as if he would like to get it. (This has been termed 'grasping with the eyes'.)

At about 4 months he tries to reach for toys, and the hands come together but he misjudges distance and overshoots or undershoots. He pulls at his clothes, and at 5 months plays with his toes. Now he can reach out and get toys, and from this time until about 12 months or so he takes almost everything to his mouth. You will notice that he goes for things with both hands, whereas in a month or two he goes for them with only one hand. If fed on a bottle he likes to help to hold it; and you can see that when he has one brick in the hand and you offer another, he drops the first: soon he will progress so that he holds on to the first. He characteristically bangs bricks on the table, or bangs the table with his hands: and reaches (at 6 to 7 months) an important milestone when he begins to pass a toy from one hand to the other. At this age he is beginning to chew. He can not only hold a biscuit but he can feed himself with it. In these early days of grasping, the cube is held in the palm of the hand and he soon drops it; but by 10 to 12 months he can hold it between the thumb and fore-finger: you can observe the intervening stages (which the paediatrician has to notice when assessing a baby's develop-ment). At 9 to 10 months he holds a brick or toy out to his mother and then refuses to part with it. At 11 or 12 months he will let it go.

At 9 or 10 months he reaches a very characteristic and important milestone: he goes for objects with his index finger, and now can pick up a pellet between the tip of his fore-finger and the tip of his thumb. He now greatly enjoys put-ting bricks into and taking them out of a basket. From 12 to 15 months he enjoys throwing one brick after another on to the floor — particularly if his sister joins in the fun and picks them up again. Soon after 12 months of age he stops taking toys to his mouth. At 13 or 14 months he is able to make a tower of two one inch cubes; by 18 months he makes a tower of three or four, by 2 years a tower of six or seven, and by 3 years a tower of ten. At 15 months he manages an ordinary cup — picking it up, drinking and putting it down without much spilling. At 18 months he turns 2 or 3 pages of a book together, but at 2 years he turns them singly; and can now put his socks, shoes and pants on. At 2½ he can thread beads and can turn a door knob or unscrew toys. He holds a pencil in the hand instead of the fist. At 3 years he manages to fasten buttons, apart from awkward ones at the back, can dress him-self almost fully, but cannot tie shoe laces. He likes to draw.

There is less variation in the development of the use of the hands than there is in the development of sitting and walk-ing. As in other aspects of development, the mentally sub-normal child is late in using his hands. With all children, much depends on the practice which his parents give him. If you fail to give him a chance to feed himself, dress himself and do other things himself, he will be held back in his dev-elopment. On the other hand, his development will be accel-erated if you give him all the wherewithall for play and for practising the use of his hands and for coordinating his vision and manipulation. Even so, some children show a special aptitude with their hands even in their early days. All children are different: but I have never seen advanced manipulative development in a mentally retarded child.

Left or right handed?

You will probably not be sure whether your child is right or left handed till he is two, three or perhaps even four. Up to the age of 2 children commonly waver between right and left handedness. Eventually around 6 per cent of British children are predominantly left handed.

Feeding and dressing

The very young baby cannot usually get his lip tightly round the mother's nipple or the teat of the bottle: hence he swallows air as he sucks — and the longer he sucks, the more air he swallows — and so he gets 'wind', for all wind which babies have is air which they have swallowed. But he soon matures, swallows less air and so gets less wind. In fact he may approximate his lips so tightly round the mother's nipple that he seems to adhere to it, having created a vacuum, and his mother inserts her finger into the corner of his mouth to release the vacuum. In the first 3 or 4 months, he may seem to push food out if it is placed on the front of the tongue. Then at 6 or 7 months he begins to chew, and as he can pick things up, he can now feed himself with a biscuit or other food. He soon wants to feed himself, holding a spoon but in the early days often turning it over at the crucial moment before it enters his mouth. He puts his fingers into his food, but you should not stop him. Some babies can feed themselves fully by about 10 months, but the average age is 15 months: that includes managing an ordinary cup without much spilling. (Long before that — from the early weeks — he would drink from a cup if it were held for him). By 2½ to 3 years he should be able to manage a knife and fork.

At 9 or 10 months he may help you to dress him by holding an arm out for a sleeve or a foot out for a shoe, or else by transferring a toy from one hand to another so that the hand can go through a sleeve. The age at which he will be able to dress himself then depends largely on the opportunity which you give him to do it for himself, and partly on his level of intelligence. At 18 months children take their shoes, socks and gloves off, and unzip a zip: at 2 years they put their shoes, socks and pants on, but probably will not be able to tie a shoe lace until they are nearly 5. One expects an average child to dress himself fully when he is 3, apart from help with buttons and shoe laces.

Bowel and bladder control

A new baby voids (relieves himself) entirely by an involuntary (reflex) action: the action is sometimes stimulated by handling him, or by a cold hand on his thighs especially after a feed. But at any age it may be possible to 'condition' him to use the pottie when he is placed on it so that when his buttocks feel the rim of the pottie he may empty the bladder. This is *not* a voluntary act. Frequently, after 9 months or so, this involuntary conditioned voiding seems to stop, so you must realise that the voiding was involuntary, otherwise you may think that he is being naughty and punish him. If you do this, there will be real difficulty. Voluntary control rarely begins before 15 months, and it often begins much later. The first sign that it is beginning is his announcement that he has wet his pants; shortly he announces when he is doing it; then he announces that he is going to do it, but there is great urgency in the early days and he cannot wait. He is not being naughty. He cannot help it. This commonly continues from 18 to 24 or 30 months of age. Many babies are mostly dry by day at 18 to 24 months, if placed on the pottie after a meal or after being out of doors, but accidents occur, especially if the child is not reminded. At 2 to 2½ years the child can pull his pants down, climb on to the lavatory seat, and do what he needs to do. He will probably be able to control his bowels before his bladder. By 24 months 1 in 2 children are usually dry at night. By 3 years, 3 of every 4 children are dry at night, with occasional mishaps, and at 5 years 9 out of 10 are dry. To put it another way, one out of every ten children still occasionally wet themselves at night at the age of five years.

Many factors affect the age at which the child controls the bowel and bladder. When a child is late in controlling the bladder, there is usually a family history of the same thing: presumably there has been delayed maturation of the relevant part of the nervous system, and this is a hereditary feature. Coercive toilet training is extremely likely to delay control: when a child is compelled to sit on the pottie when he wants to get off, or when he is punished for not using it, trouble is almost inevitable. On the other hand failure to give the child a chance to use the pottie when he wants to can also delay control. Psychological stress, any form of insecurity, may lead to delay or loss of control, especially if it occurs just at the time that control is being learnt. Punitive methods can certainly delay control, but control canot be accelerated. Psychological factors in mother or child are of great importance: efforts to make a determined child do something that he does not want to do will inevitably lead to trouble. If a great deal of fuss and anxiety is shown about toilet training, the child will refuse as an attention-seeking device. Absence of an indoor lavatory may be a factor if it is unpleasant for the child to go to the lavatory. Most mentally retarded children are slow in learning control of the bladder.

Response to sound

Though it is not always easy to demonstrate it, the young baby in his first two months can be shown to hear a sudden noise by a startle, catch in his breathing, a cry (if not already crying), stopping of crying for a second, or blinking of the eyes (p. 44). At 3 to 4 months he turns his head to sound. (This can often be demonstrated sooner.) At about 6 months he may imitate sounds. At one year he turns his head on hearing his name.

Development of understanding

Much has been said about this in the section on the development of communication. I mentioned the beginning of the smile, and then the sounds and the long 'conversation' which the child holds with his mother at 3 or 4 months when she talks to him. At 3 months he is very interested in his surroundings, and in the activities involved in housework. He becomes excited when a toy is given to him. He turns his head away when you try to clean his nose. He begins to get excited when the breast or bottle is being prepared for a feed. At 5 months he smiles at his mirror image, and looks down to the floor when he drops a toy. At 6 months he holds his arms out when he sees that his mother is going to pull him up. He expresses disapproval when a toy is removed from him and he also shows likes and dislikes of certain foods, immediately recognising something which he does not like. He enjoys games and laughs as his head is hidden in a towel; he tries to draw his mother's attention by a cough; he likes the peep-bo game.

At 7 months he begins to respond to 'No'. He pushes your hand away when you try to clean his nose. He pats his mirror image and changes his posture to see it. He laughs if you keep repeating a 'game' for him and responds to his name. He keeps his lips tightly closed if offered food which he dislikes. He reaches persistently for toys out of reach. At 8 or 9 months he characteristically 'matches' two bricks, apparently comparing them. He holds his arms in front of his face to try to prevent it being washed. He looks round a corner to see something which interests him. He enjoys playing patacake. He repeats a performance laughed at. At 9 or 10 months he helps his mother to dress him (or may positively impede her). He anticipates movements in nursery rhymes.

He deliberately drops toys so that they will be picked up. At 10 or 11 months he likes to look at picture books, and enjoys listening to a book being read to him and pictures being shown to him. He shakes his head for 'No'. At 12 months he may respond to such questions as 'where is your foot, your shoe?' From this time onwards his play becomes more complex and imaginative.

Summary

Below is a summary of milestones of development, arranged this time by age. Remember that all the ages listed for the milestones are average ones only: that all children are different: and that very few children are average in all fields of development — and that they will reach those milestones earlier or later than the ages given.

Age in months	Features of development of full-term baby
1	4—6 weeks — begins to smile at mother in response: prior to that watches her intently as she speaks to him. Held with hand under abdomen, face down, at 6 weeks holds head up momentarily in plane of the body.
2	On abdomen — lifts chin off couch. Lying on back — follows moving object near eyes. Coos as well as smiles.
3	Holds rattle placed in hand, but cannot pick it up. Hands mostly open. Held with hand under abdomen, face down, holds head up well beyond plane of body. Becomes excited when offered toy. Turns head away when mother tries to clean nose. Holds long 'conversation' with mother as she speaks to him. Squeals of pleasure. 3—4 months turns head to sound on level with ear, 18 inches away.
4	On back — hands come together in play. Pulls dress over face.

	Excited when feed is being prepared.
	Laughs aloud.
	On abdomen — chin and chest off couch.
	Definitely turns head to sound.
	Tries to reach for object, but overshoots.
5	On abdomen — bears weight on forearms.
	On back — feet to mouth. Plays with toes.
	Reaches and gets toy without it being put into hand.
	From now till 12 months or so — all objects are taken to mouth.
	Goes for objects with both hands.
	Blows raspberries. Says 'Ah goo'.
6	On abdomen — bears weight on hands, extended elbows.
	When lying on back and about to be pulled up, holds arms out to mother for her to pull.
	Lifts head up spontaneously.
	Transfers object from one hand to another.
	Sits with both hands on couch for support.
	Rolls, front to back.
	Smiles at mirror image.
	Bears full weight on legs.
	Drops one brick when offered a second.
	When toy is dropped, he looks to see where it went.
	Becomes excited on hearing footsteps.
	Food — likes and dislikes.
	May cry when stranger approaches.
	Displeasure at removal of toy.
	Laughs aloud at game when head is covered by towel: enjoys peep-bo game.
	Imitates cough, tongue protrusion.
	Draws attention by a cough.
	Begins to chew, as distinct from sucking.
7	Smiles and vocalises at mirror image.
	Rolls, back to front.
	Sits for seconds on floor without rolling over.
	Bounces when held standing.
	Bangs bricks and hands on table.
	Feeds self with biscuit,
	Goes for object with one hand.
	If he is holding one brick, retains it when second offered.
	Keeps lips closed if offered food to which he objects.
	Imitates simple movements or sound.
	Pats his mirror image.

	Responds to 'No'.
	Shows expectation in response to repetition of a stimulus.
	Says ba, da, ka.
	Pushes mother's hand away when she tries to clean his nose.
8	Sits minutes on floor without rolling over.
	Leans forward to reach things.
	Stands holding on to furniture.
	Says dada, mumum — not with meaning.
9	On abdomen — may progress backwards when trying to crawl: may crawl — pulling himself forward by his hands.
	Leans forward for objects and recovers balance.
	Pulls self to standing position.
	Holds arms over face to prevent mother cleaning his nose.
10	Goes for objects with index finger.
	Picks up pellet between tip of forefinger and tip of thumb.
	Helps mother to dress him — arm out for coat, foot for shoe.
	Plays clap hands, waves bye bye.
	Appears to compare bricks when one is in each hand.
	Walks, holding on to furniture.
	Gets from abdomen to sit and vice versa, but collapses with bump.
	Responds to words — 'where is daddy?'
	Offers parent a toy but will not let it go.
	Repeats a performance laughed at.
	Creeps — on hands and knees.
	Enjoys putting objects in and out of basket.
11	When creeping, may put foot flat on floor.
	When sitting, can twist round without falling.
	Walks, 2 hands held.
	Rolls ball to mother.
	Offers toy and lets it go.
	One word with meaning.
	Looks at book: enjoys being read to.
12	May walk like a bear, on hands and sole of foot.
	Nearly stopped taking objects to mouth.
	Begins casting — throwing one object after another on the floor.
	Points correctly to 'where is your shoe?'
	Three words with meaning.
	Knows meaning of many words.

	Nearly stopped dribbling.
	At 13 to 14 months builds tower of two one-inch cubes.
	13 months — walks a few steps, no support.
15	Kneels.
	Creeps up stairs.
	Can get from sitting to standing position.
	Holds two bricks in one hand.
	Cannot throw ball without falling.
	Manages ordinary cup — picking it up, drinking, putting it down.
	Feeds self, but may rotate spoon.
	Asks for objects by pointing.
	Imitates mother brushing, sweeping, washing up.
	May tell mother that he has wet his pants.
	Jargon — with a few interspersed words.
18	Gets up and down stairs, holding on to rail.
	Seats self in chair.
	Jumps off both feet.
	Tower of 3 or 4 one inch cubes.
	Many words.
	Throws ball without falling.
	Takes off gloves, socks: unzips.
	Spontaneous scribble. Imitates one stroke.
	Points on request to 3 or 4 parts of body.
	Points to objects in picture — when asked where is ... ?
	Turns pages, 2 or 3 at a time.
	May be dry by day, wets at night.
24	At 21 to 24 months, spontaneously joins 2 or 3 words.
	Walks backwards in imitation.
	Up and down stairs, 2 feet per step.
	Runs.
	Kicks ball without falling.
	Turns door knob: unscrews things.
	Washes and dries hands.
	Tower of 6 or 7 one inch cubes.
	Puts on shoes, socks, pants: takes them off.
	Pulls mother to show her things.
	Points to several parts of the body.
	Imitates mother drawing vertical stroke or circle.
	Turns pages of book singly.
	Dry at night if lifted.
	Asks for drink, lavatory, food.
	Repeats things said to him.
	Uses words I, me, you.
	Wraps up doll, puts it to bed.

	Does not play with other children, but likes to play on his own in their presence.
30	Tower of 8 one inch cubes.
	Talks incessantly.
	Makes two strokes for a cross.
	Knows full name, sex.
	Attends to toilet needs without help except wiping.
	Threads beads.
	Knows one colour.
36	Jumps off bottom step.
	Goes upstairs, one foot per step, down two feet per step.
	Stands for seconds on one foot.
	Rides tricycle.
	Helps to set table.
	Tower of 10 one inch cubes.
	Dresses and undresses fully apart from some buttons and apart from shoe laces.
	Copies circle, imitates a cross.
	Knows some nursery rhymes.
	Counts to 10.
	Joins in play with other children.
42	Imaginary play companions.
48	Goes downstairs, one foot per step.
	Skips on one foot.
	Buttons clothes fully.
	Copies a cross.
	Constant questioning.
	Tells tall stories.
	Imaginative play with doll.
54	Copies square.
60	Skips on both feet.
	Ties shoe laces.
	Knows four colours.
	Compares two weights.

When should I ask the doctor's advice?

It is impossible to lay down any hard and fast rule about this. I have emphasised the wide variation in different fields of development, and have pointed out that it is impossible to draw the line between normal and abnormal. But it is true to say that the further away from the average a child is in any aspect of development — the age of sitting, walking, talking, controlling the bladder, or any other skill — the greater the possibility that there is a cause for it. You should certainly seek advice if your child is later than usual in talking, in case there is some degree of deafness. You should seek advice if your child is much later than average in controlling the bladder — but remember that there are especially wide variations in this, commonly a family characteristic: but there is the possibility, particularly in girls, that there is an infection in the urinary tract, which can be treated. Certainly if boy or girl has constant dribbling of urine you should consult your doctor urgently and ask to see a paediatric expert, because there may be an abnormality which can be treated.

How can I help his development?

A child's level of intelligence (IQ) can be very considerably lowered in a bad home and considerably raised in a good home. In this section I have tried to put together some of the things that you, as a good mother, can do to help to bring the best out of your child and raise his IQ. I have already discussed the other essentials to this aim — the ways of helping a child in his physical and emotional development, which are going to be of such vital importance to his future: for you will aim not just to help him to achieve his maximum potential (which may not be high) but to help him to be a nice, happy healthy person. He may or may not be endowed with many talents; what matters is what he does with those talents, and that is where you will help him to achieve his best. You must not expect too much of him; you certainly must not expect more than his intellectual endowment will permit; neither must you expect him to be perfect, because he will not be. It is important that you should be ambitious for him, for if you expect little of him, he is likely to achieve little: but it is disastrous to be overambitious, to expect too much of him, for that will lead you to be disappointed in him, and it will lead him to feel insecure and unhappy. Some parents become really tense about their child's progress: they try to teach him when he has no interest in learning, or to concentrate on his lessons when his powers of concentration are poor, or when his real interests lie elsewhere. One should never exert pressure on him to learn: the important thing is that he should enjoy learning and want to learn.

It is disastrous to be disappointed in a child — in his intellectual development or in his behaviour. In any case, you should not be so sure of his apparent lack of promise. There are numerous examples of children who were thought by parents and teachers to be totally lacking in promise, and who nevertheless acquired world fame.

Some parents argue that it is soon enough for a child to begin learning when he starts school: but they are very wrong. Children learn to learn, learn to enjoy learning, at home, long before they are old enough to go to school. Many think that the first two or three years of life are vital for a child's future ability to learn, and so are vital for his school days. Teachers are presented with 5-year-olds who have been modelled by their parents, and who reveal what the parents have done to them and for them.

Some are afraid that they may 'overstrain' their child if they allow him to learn to read before he starts school if he shows that he is ready for it: to some the idea of giving a child 'educational toys' is totally wrong. There is no ground for such fears.

It would, however, be wrong to think that the earlier a child learns something, the better: what is important is that he should be helped to learn as soon as he is ready to learn. As soon as children show that they are developmentally ready for new skills, they should be given the opportunity to practise them. When they show that they can chew (usually at 6 or 7 months), they should be given solids, like a biscuit, crust or piece of apple, to chew: if they are deprived of such foods to chew, there may be real difficulty later, so that they refuse solids. They should be allowed to help to hold the bottle or cup, to use the spoon and later the knife and fork, to sit, stand

and walk, to dress themselves and to attend to their toilet needs, as soon as they are ready: they take great pleasure in practising these new skills. The principle of the Montessori method of teaching is just this — to help children to learn various skills as soon as they are ready, when they most enjoy learning and practising them.

You cannot expect your baby to learn much if he is lying in a pram all day with nothing but a brick wall to see — or if you leave him for hours on end in a playpen. If he is going to learn he will need your time, and a lot of it: he will need you to talk to him, play with him and read to him.

Toys and play

By play children learn and benefit emotionally, physically and mentally. They derive satisfaction from practising their new skills: they enjoy playing; they acquire a sense of achievement: they are saved from boredom; they can express their feelings (e.g. with the hammer toy): as they get older they are helped to lose their shyness, they learn to play with others, to obey the rules, to be honest, to be loyal and unselfish: they learn their responsibility to others; and they learn that if they fail in these respects others will not play with them. They gain from exercise out of doors. They learn new motor skills: they learn to coordinate eye and hand: they learn how things work, how things are made: they observe, use their imagination, and develop their special interests and aptitudes.

There are several principles with regard to selection of play material for children. The selection will depend on the child's age, aptitudes and interests, and to some extent on the sex. Toys must be safe, non-flammable, have no sharp corners which will injure a child. They must have fast colours, and be firmly made so that they do not readily break and cause injury: for instance, a small plastic trumpet in the mouth might break and cause serious damage to the mouth or throat. In the case of the young child, there must be no detachable parts (such as the eyes of a stuffed animal) which could be inhaled. Cheap stuffed teddies may be dangerous if poor material for stuffing has been used.

Parents have to be constantly alert to possible dangers which the child cannot anticipate. Pointed pencils and especially indelible ones can seriously injure an eye. Fireworks should never be allowed except under close supervision; they cause numerous tragedies such as severe burns or serious damage to an eye. Money should be spent more wisely.

Outdoor equipment may have its dangers. The swing can cause grave injury when a small child runs behind it; a roundabout can cause similar injury. Beware of drain holes in the pathway which a child may use for his tricycle or bicycle. Bows and arrows should never be bought for a child: they may cause serious injury to the eye. One must not overprotect: but one must prevent serious injuries which the child cannot be expected to foresee.

Money for toys should be spent wisely: highly expensive dolls are not appreciated more by a girl than are much less expensive ones — especially those dolls with clothes which can be changed. Many mothers can in a short time make such clothes for an inexpensive doll. Expensive mechanical toys are a waste of money: for the most part they do not enable the child to use his imagination, to build, to practise his skills. They tend to please the father rather than the boy, and when the boy misuses a mechanical toy (e.g. pushing a clockwork engine on the floor) the father is liable to become angry. Some equipment, such as a Wendy house, or a climbing frame, is very expensive: there is a ready supply of the expensive equipment for children, (including frames, playpens etc) on the second hand market.

Fathers (and some mothers) buy toys of aggression for their children — toy guns and pistols. It is uncertain whether they do any harm: but they certainly give the child little opportunity to use his imagination and to learn from them.

It is a mistake to give too many toys at a time: it is much more sensible to put some away and change over at intervals.

If possible, let your child have a play room, or at least a cupboard of his own where he learns to keep his own property.

In the early days the parent joins in the play, helping him with new toys, such as Lego, but letting him use his own imagination thereafter, instead of constantly suggesting what he should do with the toy. Independent play should be encouraged, not prevented by a parent who will not leave the child alone.

Toys in the first year

When buying a rattle, be sure that it is a light one: I have seen rattles which I regard as too heavy, in that they would harm the eye if the baby hit the eye with one.

When the baby has developed far enough to reach out and get toys (average age 5 months), a wide variety of small objects are useful — bobbins, wood curtain rings, a plastic cup with spoon, bath toys and small bricks. One inch cubes are a suitable size for his hand. At 10 months or so children enjoy taking things out of containers and putting them in again, and a basket or box is useful. A small round tin containing lentils or small pebbles may be popular as long as there is no risk that the top will come off, when the baby might inhale one of the pebbles. Cuddly toys are likely to be popular. In the last three months of the first year picture books made of firm card are liked by small children: they can be left with these, but they are distinct from books which a mother shows to her child, containing pictures or nursery rhymes.

Toys after the first year

The best single present for a child after his first year is a sack of bricks of different sizes and shapes; it gives immense scope for his imagination. I strongly advise you against buying clockwork and other mechanical toys which give little scope for creative play. Other useful toys include push and pull toys (especially those with detachable parts), interlocking bricks and toys of the Lego type, wooden or plastic toys which can be taken apart and put together again, simple formboards (e.g. with three cut-out holes of different shapes into which appropriate blocks fit), simple jigsaws — commencing with 6-piece ones, increasing in number of pieces as the child becomes ready for more difficult ones, a posting box with slots of different sizes and shapes into which appropriate blocks are 'posted', construction kits, hammer toys, picture dominoes, picture matching games, colour-matching games (e.g. wools of different colours), animal templates, tracing books, cardboard coins, bead threading equipment, a lacing card (celluloid with holes for lacing and design making), pyramid rings, nesting boxes, a magnet and magnetic shapes, a gyroscope, plastic letters and figures to match on corresponding cards, a plastic clock with removable numbers, plastic farms.

Children from about 15 months characteristically copy the mother in her chores of cooking, washing up, dusting and cleaning. Children therefore enjoy the appropriate material — for the doll's teaparty, a doll's house, brushes, a toy carpet sweeper — and the opportunity to wash up after the doll's party. An empty shoe box can be fashioned into a house or garage with doors and windows. Blunt scissors are suitable after the third birthday.

Drawing, painting material, plasticine or similar modelling material is useful. A blackboard with coloured chalks or an easel with painting and drawing material may occupy many hours of constructive play. A Wendy house, perhaps with a shop, is also likely to be much used: a dressing up box fits in well here.

Out-of-doors equipment includes a tricycle (by three years of age), or a sandpit. A paddling pool with suitable bowls, watering can, jugs and rubber tubing is excellent provided that the necessary supervision is available so that no one drowns in it. Most of the expensive equipment can be made by a handyman or bought second hand.

Many cities have a toy library, often attached to the Children's Section of a public library.

Firms which supply suitable play equipment for the pre-school child include:

Mothercare.
Lego.
Kiddicraft.
Early Learning Centre, 25 King's Road, Reading.
Fisher Price.
E.J. Arnold, Butterly Street, Leeds.
(Ask for the 'Offspring' catalogue).
Charles and Son, Clerkenwell Green, London, EC1.
Philip and Tracey, High Street, Fulham, London SW6.
Wilkane, Eastbourne, Sussex.
Educational Supply Association, Pinnacles, Harlow, Essex.
(This firm has a booklet entitled *Getting Ready to Read* which lists toys which teach eye hand coordination, size and shape.)
Galt Toys, 30 Great Marlborough Street, London Wl.

I suggest you ask these firms for their catalogue.

Books

Any time from about nine months of age children like to be shown 'books: objects are pointed out and soon the child points objects out on request. In the first place, look for books with simple pictures showing only one object at a time — pictures of common objects in colour. A scrap book made by you is a good beginning and can be readily made from colour magazines. Children learn a great deal from the picture books: they may show little interest at first but soon become very interested. The child is shown pictures of objects, buildings, farms etc and is then shown the real thing. He soon begins to enjoy the rhythm of nursery rhymes: he learns to listen to stories, and then to use his imagination. Many mothers begin to read to their children much too late. I have known professional parents who never thought of reading to their children before they were three or four years of age. Ten- to twelve-month-old babies of average intelligence enjoy being shown pictures in books, like to hear simple stories and nursery rhymes, and learn a lot from them.

There is a wide scope in books for the preschool child: they include the Ladybird series, Gay Colour books, Picture Puffin Books, e.g. *This Little Puffin, Rhyme Time* (Barbara Ireson), *Over and Over Again* (Barbara Ireson and Christopher Rowe),Books for Me Series (Abelard), Puffin Easy Readers (e.g. *Ben's Fish, Lillapig*),Picture Lion Series (*Tiger that came to Tea; Mog the Forgetful Cat; When Willey went to the Wedding*), Topsy and Tim books (Blackie), Dick Bruna Books (Methuen), Altha books (Dinosoar Publications) Scamp series (Arnold), Homestart books, Methuen Caption Books and Read it Yourself Books (and other Caption Books), and the Beatrix Potter series. The public library children's section will include many of these and many others. Firms which specialise in Children's books include:- E.J. Arnold, Butterly Street, Leeds. A. Wheaton, Exeter. Children's Book Shop, The Broad, Oxford.

Music and records

Children enjoy the various records now available, for example BBC songs for children for action, dancing and singing; and they may be given a chance to hear suitable music on the radio.

Some vital needs and steps to achievement

I firmly believe that if a child is to achieve his best, the following are the essential requirements:

1. *Help him to learn to want to learn* and to enjoy learning. This means that he must be helped to learn, and shown how to learn. It means explaining things and showing him how things work. It means encouraging him to be curious, to investigate, to ask. It means avoiding reprimanding him for 'being into everything'. It means avoiding punishing him for trying to find out, especially when the consequences of his

quest are unfortunate because he could not anticipate the consequences.

2. *Encourage him to ask questions*. The best way to encourage him to ask questions is to try to answer them. You will have difficulty in answering some of them ('When will it be to-morrow?' 'What is a soul?'. 'What is a Holy Ghost?' 'Why is it raining') A colleague was asked 'Draw a difference. Why can't you draw a difference?'. If you cannot answer, try with him to find out. Set the example of trying to find out. Show the older pre-school child the purpose of the Reference Library and how one finds things out in it. The trouble is that many parents resent having their authority questioned. It is just disastrous to answer 'Why?' with 'Because I said so', 'That's enough from you', 'I won't have any back chat' or 'Not another word'.

Praise him for trying to find out — and never discourage. It gives him a sense of satisfaction and achievement to find out. Do not let him fail: teach him persistence — to try, try again. Failure is liable to discourage: success breeds success. But in his building operations let him make mistakes, so that he learns.

3. *Encourage him to think and create*. Originality and creativity are vital if he is to be successful. Do not discourage him or ridicule him or reprimand him for fantasy play and 'tall stories'. Let him see you use your imagination and think of stories and tell them to him.

4. *Teach him that we all have a right to have our own views and ideas*, but that our ideas and thoughts are not necessarily the only ones or the correct ones. Respect his ideas. Respect his right to reject your opinions. Try to teach him to think round things, to seek other explanations. Teach him to question statements made in newspaper and radio advertisements. When you ask him a question, you should want him to say 'It all depends . . . , to show that he sees various possibilities, that he is beginning to seek and weigh evidence.

5. *Give him every possible chance to acquire knowledge*. You may show him pictures (e.g. of a railway station, farm) in

a book — and then show him the real thing. Show him pictures of flowers, animals — and then let him see real flowers and animals in the country. Show him how things grow in the garden. Teach him to recognise shapes, sizes, colours, texture. Teach him to learn cause and effect. Teach him to recognise similarities, dissimilarities, relationships, associations. Teach him to observe. The 'I spy' game is a useful one for this (and a useful way of profitably spending a long car journey). Teach him to acquire the concept of numbers, by counting steps, objects in the supermarket, conkers. Give him a toy clock with detachable numbers which he fits into the right place.

6. *Encourage his interest and aptitudes.* If he wants to collect things, help him. If he wants to draw, help him by giving him the necessary materials.

7. *Try to teach accuracy, thoroughness, persistence.* Try not to let him accept defeat or failure easily.

8. *Try to teach him to take responsibility,* to be helpful, to take the lead.

9. *Encourage accuracy of speech.* Always avoid baby talk, which the child has to unlearn before he learns proper speech. Give him opportunities to enlarge his vocabulary by pointing objects out to him — in books, and in real life. Encourage him to understand ambiguity in speech, for example 'I saw a dead sheep walking across the moor'. Set the example of careful speech. Talk to him. Read to him. Do not leave him out of adult conversation. I deplore the common practice in some countries abroad (and sometimes in Britain) of sending children out of the room when visitors come. Let the children listen and join in.

Possible criticism

It might be suggested that all the above suggestions are designed to try to make one's child a genius, or that my suggestions are relevant only to a bright child. That is not true. But the less bright child is likely to have less good powers of concentration than a bright one, and it is vital that you do not try to compel a less bright child — or any child — to concentrate, to look at books, to construct objects with his construction set, if he does not want to, or if he has a short attention span. Efforts to push a child further than his abilities will permit will inevitably lead to insecurity and unpleasantness.

What about the mentally gifted child? Everything which I have said applies to him. Remember that his physical powers (e.g. in sport) are likely to lag behind his intellectual powers. Above all, encourage him in his special interests. Stretch him — give him more and more difficult tasks without letting him fail. Try to avoid merely filling in his time. Direct your attention to quality rather than quantity so that he has to think, to persevere, to try to create.

A glimpse forward to early school age.

The following, in brief, are some suggestions for helping the young school child to optimum achievement.

When he is about to start school, implant the expectation that he is going to enjoy school in the work, play and friendships. Do not suggest that he will have trouble in settling down by the 'You'll be all right, Jack' attitude, which will immediately suggest to him that there is something to fear.

Recognise the importance of education. Avoid unnecessary school absence. Far too many children are kept off school totally unnecessarily, so that their education suffers. It is absurd to keep a child off school for a trivial cold, cough or wheeze. Before keeping him off school on account of any symptom, decide in your own mind why you think that it would be better for him to miss school than to attend it — against the loss which he will suffer by school absence.

Continue to give him all possible opportunities to learn. Encourage his use of the library. Spend money wisely on books or magazines: do not waste money on so-called 'comics' which will give him no help at all.

Do not fill up his spare time too much with organised pursuits. Leave him time for devoting to his own interests and aptitudes. Beware of letting him take spare time work to earn money: it must not take him away from more useful pursuits.

Interest in sport is to be encouraged: but on occasion it may be necessary to ensure that he does not devote so much time to it that his work suffers.

See that it is just automatic for him to do his homework after his meal. Do not do it for him. It is usually unwise to check it for him. Help him with it only on special occasions, not as a routine.

See, if possible, that he has a room in which to do his homework, away from a radio or TV set.

Do not make unreasonable demands on the school for special privileges for him because he is unusually bright. Leave it to the school. Do not show overprotection by trying to get him excused from physical exercise or sport. Overprotection also includes taking him to school when he is old enough to be independent and to go without you.

When necessary, guide him with regard to choice of subjects at school. Only in the most exceptional circumstances should he be prevented from pursuing his special interests.

Keep contact with the school, consulting the teachers if difficulties arise or decisions as to the future have to be made.

If the question of choice of school arises, choose on the basis of his ability, interest, personality and desires. It is only reasonable that his own strong desires should be considered: this applies particularly if there is a question of sending him to a boarding school. The choice of school should on no account be made on the basis of its snob value. I have seen many children (especially girls) suffer greatly from the educational point of view by being sent to a third-rate boarding school, for snob reasons, when they would have had far greater opportunity for achievement in a good State school.